Buffalo Stampede: Book One

The Birds Sang a Sad Song

David C. Craig

ISBN-13: 978-1499788792
ISBN-10: 1499788797

Dedication:

First, this book is dedicated to Mary Connealy who refused to let me give up. Writing this book was very difficult and I scrapped the first two attempts. Mary gently prodded me on. "People need this book," she repeatedly said and said again until the last page was finished. Thank you, Mary.

It is also dedicated to the wonderful people in our local church family who have been equally supportive, understanding and loving, and who, like Mary, pushed me to the finish line. Thank you, dear friends.

Contents:

Chapter 1
On the Run

Morning sun came dancing into the room, leaping from dust speck to dust speck until all was filled with the fluid motion of light. The half filled glass of water on the nightstand kicked up its heels in a radiant rainbow splashed along the wall. Picture frames upon the opposite wall blinked glittering squares of light back at the sun. Life sprang from the light and vibrantly sang, "It's a glorious day! Arise! Arise! Arise! Capture the moment! Seize the Day! Grab hold of the joy of living!"

That is a fair to middlin' opening, I guess. It could do with refinement. All writing can do with refinement. That is the bugaboo that writers constantly face. I could turn that phrase better. Oh, yeah, that word would fit more appropriately here. My, I wish I had thought of that before it went into print. Anyway, that is a fair to middlin' opening paragraph for a book that is actually going in quite a different direction.

Certainly there will be less light. There will be less exuberant singing. Rainbows will not really spring up along a wall. Corners will be dark. Pictures will not dazzle and the glass will really be half empty. The glory of the day will be questionable and certainly, very certainly, arising with expectations of radiant light and joyful song will be muted to simply arising.

As a child I always liked the song, "Home on the Range". There they are; the deer and the antelope playing. Do you see them? Do you see the buffalo? They are roaming quietly, nibbling grass, nuzzling each other. The sun shines. The birds sing. The insects hum in the grass. The bees buzz from prairie flower to prairie flower. How idyllic. How beautiful. How serene. OK, so there is a little light, a little joy - a little joie de vivre. If into every life a little rain must fall, then I suppose into every life a little sun must shine. I apologize in advance for any such outbreaks of unexpected moments of joy.

I was actually getting to the buffalo. I love buffalos. I took my family to South Dakota to see them and we parked our van in the middle of herd of them and I just basked at their beauty. My family was not nearly so enamored. The kids were rather pulling back from the windows with unsmiling faces. Granted buffalo are far bigger than children. They are far bigger than I. My children were much more fascinated by the guy on the motorcycle behind us who was also stuck, stuck was their word not mine, in the middle of the buffalo herd. Finally the herd all moseyed off and we went on our way, the children gladly and me reluctantly. It was nice to see the buffalo quiet and peaceful and up close.

The reason for that is simple. Usually when I see buffalo there are a million of them. They aren't just in a herd of a hundred or so. The plains are covered with them just like they were before the great westward expansion of the United States. But when I see them, they are not grazing. They are stampeding and I am in their path. There is no giant rock to hide behind. There is no ditch to slip into where they might actually jump over me instead of on me. There is just me and them. There are a lot of them and they are in a hurry. And I am in their way. There is more to come on that point later.

I worked hard on a vehicle for this book. Buffalo are kind of a 19th century thing. Therefore I envisioned a fictionalized adaptation of events to a 19th century setting. I can still see little Daniel Cooper standing on the banks of the Missouri gazing with expectation and fear at the vast prairie beyond. Driven by despair and hope, fear and need, angst and energy he would set out with others but still all alone on the great western adventure. Minimalized by the endless sky and great prairie-grass sea he would discover the essence of his utter aloneness and yet find the resilience that only those trampled by a buffalo stampede can understand. When we meet Daniel Cooper elsewhere in this book remember this trembling adolescent on an adult journey.

But another more practical vehicle also exits. It is the vehicle of reality. It is the vehicle of a mindset more 19th century than contemporary but still placed in a modern setting. It is of a boy whose imagination is set backwards more than forwards. It is of a time when television heroes were cowboys, who in the absurdity of dramatization drove in cars and talked on telephones while also riding their galloping horses to gunfights. It was the age when every boy wanted to be Davy Crockett or Daniel Boone or Roy Rogers. It was an age when America's past was made of solid gold and her heroes were truly heroes. Good guys wore white and always won.

There was another darker essence to the age. It was an age when all of America, perhaps all the world, was running away from reality. The Second World War had just been won. The Nazis and the Japanese had been defeated, but the human cost of war, the horror of the atomic bomb, the reality of new enemies had everyone on the run. We were running from memories that wouldn't fade. We were running from horrors that could instantly engulf and destroy us. We were running from painful memories of the Great Depression. We were trying to buy our way out of the fear and memory of want and the horrors of "what if". We had put our foot on the accelerator pedal of both forgetfulness and acquisition and it was stuck in overdrive. Safety was to be found in 19th century greatness and 20th century technology. At least some technology was idolized as savior. The other was feared as doom.

America was on the go. The past may have been our anchor, but the future was our hope. Daniel Boone never had it so luxurious in his travels as those who could ride in the big finned cars of the late 50's. He might have been the example of strong will and determination, but those cars were the testimony that we weren't going back to what had been. We were going to send a rocket to the moon and we were going to drive an equally sleek and powerful rocket down the street. Nothing could speak quite so clearly to the end of a mindset of deprivation than was shouted along the streets by a gleaming 1959 Impala.

Gradually Davy Crockett and the Great Depression were jointly consigned to the past and America erupted into the future of hope and great expectations. Seemingly the race against traumatic memories was won. We had run hard and fast enough to escape the orbit of our own history. We warped into time travel mode and landed in the most fantastic and hopeful place of all – Camelot. Although Camelot had only been make-believe, no one wanted to believe that.

It was no time to be a Debby Downer. Doubt and despair were evil twins from an evil past. Besides, the wonders of modern medicine had eradicated the need for either with the choice of happy pills or happy therapy. Those who weren't optimists were either reactionary or maybe even communists. It was a wonderful age built on the faulty fabric of human achievement and it would soon collapse from the very weight of its own false expectations. Wars would not cease. Despair of the Great Depression was discovered to be alive and well for an entire segment of the American population. A wave of a new kind of depression began to sweep over the coddled children of the age of hope. Money and speed and illusions had failed to make them happy. If those things couldn't bring happiness, what could? A collapse of hope swept in on the heels of the greatest prosperity and advancements America had ever known.

It collapsed as a young boy came of age with a disease most unspeakable. Perhaps this dread disease was only a mirror reflection of the new age of realism that succeeded the age of excessive optimism. Perhaps it was only adolescent angst that would dissolve with maturity. Perhaps, even worse, it was a disorder conjured from the depths of ancient and forsaken theology. Perhaps it was a device or ploy for self aggrandizement. Perhaps it was many things or anything or nothing at all, but it certainly was not understood and even less was it a topic for discussion.

The young man coming of age stared sullenly at the clock on the classroom wall. Perhaps by sheer power of the will and a little telekinesis he could propel it faster to the 3:30 bell. There would be no work tonight in the biology lab. Mr. Turner, the only teacher or for that matter person in the school that knew he existed, had said they were done for the week having finished last night with the catalogue of invertebrates in the specimen room. It would be straight home tonight, a desire not altogether in favor with the young man.

Without the benefit of either will power or telekinesis the bell rang and the young man slouched his way out of the room and the belly of the horrible beast. Once off the school grounds he lit up his much desired cigarette and hoped he looked cooler than he felt. Maybe Taylor would see him walking down the street with his cigarette lying carelessly in the corner of his mouth. Maybe she would see him as a cool dude, a real stud, instead of the loser who sat silently in the back of each class. Maybe if he walked by her house she would really see that he wasn't the failure that others painted him as being. Maybe she would come out and say "Hi" and he could delay the long walk home to his dope addled mother. Maybe his dad would be at his girlfriend's house and not home to torment him. Maybe was make-believe, a world of false hope, and so he continued his slouching walk down the street. Through the prism of sudden and unexpected tears he saw clearly the memories he had created for himself – the story with which he could live.

Chapter 2
The River

Daniel Cooper stood at the river's edge. Across that muddy water of the great Missouri lay his future. As he set his gaze on the swift current he caught himself for a moment, just a brief moment, imagining himself becoming one with the great flow of the river. The river had great value to the people who lived along it. It had great value to the hope and destiny of his great nation. In it he too could have value. The siren song rolled away and Daniel shook himself. No, he demanded his thoughts to refocus, your future isn't in the river; it's across the river.

Shaking from that brief and unexpected thought, Daniel brought his attention clearly to the opposite shore. Over there the past would be gone. Over there all the sorrows would be washed away in the sunlight dancing on the prairie. Over there was life. He shuddered again as he glanced once more at the muddy river. Being part of that river was death. What had compelled him to think of death? Why had he found, even for a moment, such peace in the thought? He hurried away from his thoughts and the river's edge.

He reached in his pocket and grasped nervously at his liberty half eagle. It was still there, just as it was each time he felt for it. It was the bounty of his future and the curse of his past. With each touch of the precious gold piece he was confronted with conflicting emotions of hope and regret. No, he insisted, it wasn't regret. It was something else, something intangible but more than regret. His Pa had said it was shame, but no, it was not that either. It was, he thought, deeper than shame and sadder than regret. It just didn't have a name.

Miss Sally, now hers had a name. Her husband Tom called it Melancholia and that was why, Daniel smiled; he still had his half eagle. Tom was sure that the clear blue sky of the west would cheer her and make her better. Tom and Sally had set out from Toledo, Ohio which had burgeoned into a small city connecting the west with the east. The Erie Canal had brought Toledo alive and changed Tom's farm into a much demanded piece of property for urban expansion. Sally had always struggled with the frequent cloudiness that backed up off the lake and had been furthered troubled by the advent of so many people. Tom said that Sally had once been gay, but she had grown more withdrawn and looked forward to a quieter place out west. They left behind three small graves where each of their children who had died in infancy were buried.

That's what Job had said would have been a better fate for him, Daniel reflected on a sermon by Reverend Stout. To die in infancy and not see the sorrows of life that had been Job's hope. Daniel had once thought it was strange how anyone would want to escape life. Then with a sudden tug of mind he amended his thought. That was how he had once thought, but then he had learned something about sorrow.

What's the matter with me today! Daniel thought he had screamed the words out loud, but nobody passing by him seemed to have noticed. He started to run, but then became fearful of creating a scene. Walking at a brisker pace he headed for the camp of those families preparing to cross the Missouri tomorrow on their way west. Independence was a bigger town than the village near which he had grown up. Suddenly he felt as trapped as Miss Sally. Maybe Melancholia was contagious like measles. He slowed his steps and fingered his coin. No, he couldn't spend it. He had to stay with Tom and Miss Sally.

Gaining control of his emotions he walked with slower and steadier tread. But he didn't long to get to the camp too quickly and began to look around the thriving town that would help send him on his way. There was the general mix of stores to be found anywhere. They didn't interest him. He had to keep the half eagle safe. He came to the school and paused to watch the children at play. They all seemed so happy. Everyone was engaged in the activity. A knot formed in his stomach. That was what he had always wanted each day at his school. He wanted to be involved with the other children at recess, but he hadn't. He had stood on the side and watched.

He remembered Billy Logan. Billy was everyone's favorite. Daniel remembered planning every day to go up to Billy and say, Can I play too? Every night he would dream that the next day would be the day. Every day he would go home and say, tomorrow I will. Daniel's reverie was broken as a teacher came outside and rang her bell. The children lined up quickly and quietly to go inside. He watched them and imagined the door of the school as the mouth of some great and horrible beast. The children were all going in to be eaten as he had been eaten day by day.

Daniel relapsed into thought. Mr. Innes stood before his eyes and glared at him. "Daniel, what kind of work is this?" he stormed. "Were there not a hundred problems I gave you to do? Why are only ten done?" He raised the switch off his desk. "A good answer, young man; step forth with a good answer." Daniel's answer was the same one that he had given in his mind to Mr. Innes yesterday and the day before and the multitude of days before that. But no answer had ever come from his mouth. His face burned a fiery red, as would his seat very soon at the end of Mr. Innes's switch. He could neither stammer out a word nor move without being pulled from his seat with a jerk from Mr. Innes's strong hand. It was only the prelude of what was to come again later at Pa's hand. Daniel could feel the fire coming to his face again and turned away from the schoolyard. For a moment, a fleeting moment, he thought again of the river.

Daniel continued to stroll in a roundabout direction toward the camp. His eyes saw things and sent messages to his feet, but his mind returned to the flat lands along the Wabash River in Indiana. The images came clearly. There was a haggard woman standing by the fireplace of their cabin. She was stirring stew in the cast iron kettle with one hand and balancing a crying baby on her hip with the other. A little girl with a tattered dress and snarled ashen hair was laying the table with the wooden plates and spoons. A loaf of bread and knife were set in the middle of the table. Two small windows let in a dim light that fell on the dirt floor and revealed two wooden chairs and a long bench. In the farthest corner a quilt made by the haggard woman was spread neatly over the low slung bed with its mattress of straw wrapped in cotton cloth.

Then heavy footsteps entered through the open door. "Daniel," the firm voice spoke without any affection, "come here." Mr. Innes had sent his message round, of that Daniel was sure. Maybe he could get by with just doing an extra hour of wood cutting and not another lickin'. At any rate there was no appetite left for bread and stew which he would still force himself to eat so that he could work again tomorrow. But Pa had other ideas today.

"Daniel," he began, and it almost seemed that he was trying not to cry, "Daniel, you have been a disappointment. There is no point in sending you to school again tomorrow or any other day hereafter." Daniel remembered distinctly that he missed the next part of the lecture. At the news of no more school his heart both sank and sang. He would never get his chance to ask Billy if he could play too. He would never again have the joy; at least he expected it to be joy, of playing with other children. All the plans of all the nights of just talking to Billy would come to naught. The failure of empty dreams grabbed his stomach with a lurch.

But, he countered, there was no more Mr. Innes. There was no more doing one hundred problems when he knew perfectly well how to do them and then taking the blame for ignorance when he wasn't. There would be no more giggles from his classmates as the switch landed on his backside for the twentieth time. There would be no more assumptions that he couldn't read just because he couldn't read in front of the class. There would be no more false assumptions that he was just a fool because he never spoke up. There was freedom and hope and the possibility to really begin to learn something without pain and with great enjoyment.

His attention was again turned to Pa's lecture. "From now on you will help me here on the farm every day. You will learn what it means to fail at education and have nothing but sore hands and a sore back for playing the fool every day at school. Maybe that and a good lickin' will get your mind in order. You are old enough to become a responsible person. You haven't shown it yet, but I'll work you and lick you and pray you into a man so help me God." With the lecture and a good lickin' they had gone in to supper.

Daniel shook his head and the images faded. His mind connected with his eyes again and he saw the church standing on the corner. Another spasm of pain gripped his stomach. The Reverend Stout had worked hard to assist Pa in Daniel's reformation. Daniel had always loved Sunday go to meeting. They sang exuberant songs and learned new ones each year from those who had gone to a brush arbor meeting. Reverend Stout could thunder like God Almighty Himself. He saw the power of God and the power of the devil at work as strongly as if he were Peter preaching beside the sea. The devil was certainly at work. He was at work in laziness. He was at work in the sloth of youth. He was at work in those who moped and listed instead of trusting more and more in Jesus. The devil was hard at work and he was itching to catch the lazy, the indolent and the weak hearted by their nose and their toes and take them all with him to his eternal abode of fire.

As the next four years of Daniel's life passed after he was removed from school, Reverend Stout had preached harder and harder and his eyes often flashed in Daniel's direction. Those years had seen a change in Daniel. Instead of becoming the man his father envisioned, he had begun to shrink within himself. Slowly his mind had turned more to see the clouds instead of the sun, to see the winter instead of the spring. In his heart he knew he should be thankful for everything the Reverend said he should be thankful for. But in his head he couldn't blot out the storms and see the goodness of wet earth bringing forth new life. He would find himself unawares standing by the wood pile crying like a little girl. He never knew why the birds had begun to sing only sad songs. But the Reverend knew. He knew that the devil now had Daniel by the nose and by the toes and was leading him to his own fiery end.

That was it exactly. Those were his Pa's last words to him just a month ago. "Daniel, you have not become a man. You have become the moodiest crying sissy of a boy that was ever planted on God's good clean earth. I fear for your everlasting soul, but I am not going to go on feeding it until the day of perdition." With that he had handed Daniel the half eagle coin and his few clothes already wrapped in a bundle that he had brought from the house. There were not to be good-byes to the haggard lady with a new baby on her hip or to the dirty girl with snarled ashen hair or to the sorry looking grave of the child already passed on.

Daniel had stood staring at Pa and then walked slowly down the lane and headed west. In his bundle he found a loaf of Ma's bread and he had lived on that for three days. Then he had met Tom and Sally Miller. They were heading west and Tom felt he needed someone to help with the team and wagon so he could spend more time with Miss Sally. Daniel accepted the offer and they fed him and let him sleep under the wagon each night. Now they were waiting for him. Before he turned to go he looked at the church steeple and prayed, "O God Almighty, can I not have a place with you anymore? Can I not escape the devil's hold on me? Can you not just give me another day when the sun shines, the birds sing and I don't cry?" Without a backward glance he returned to the Miller's wagon.

Chapter 3
Three Pieces of Paper & A Blank Sheet

The young man coming of age shook the fantasy from his mind. He relived the chapter often and it had become as much a part of him as if it were reality. But today was reality, a new reality. He watched as the scenery of the flat southern Illinois landscape rolled by. While he had been adding chapters to his life, he had not added new chapters to the memories he created.

How would I write the last four years in a book, he thought. Not a book of the past where safe memories could be stored, but a book of the present without the ending yet written. Writing had become his means to survive. It didn't matter what he had to write as long as he could write. He had done newspaper articles, joined a writer's club and built a portfolio of his work. Adults who read the local paper knew his articles but they were an unknown quantity to his peers. The writer's club was in a nearby city and his portfolio was for himself alone. Alone remained a defining word; his circle had widened, but not far. But he had actually come far. He took out his notepad and wrote a quick title, "Three pieces of paper and a blank sheet".

The first piece of paper had omitted his name but it had been critically important just the same. His parents had divorced and no one had put his name on the list of children for whom they sought custody. That omission meant he was free to choose. Not wanting to be shoved further in the background by his upcoming new step brothers and sisters, he had chosen to live with his mother. He had actually asserted a choice that meant change and change was as fearful to him as any demon. There was a new school with all the potential of new success or a repeat of old failures. Location, he had discovered, made no difference unless inner change came with outer change. So, he had largely remained on the outside.

His biggest fear had become that someone would learn of his mother's condition. How could he bring a friend home to that? The second piece of paper had resolved the problem for him. His mother had been nearly killed in an accident arising from her drug addled state. He had been called out of class and driven to the hospital which was three cities away. Yes, she would live, but no, she would not be out soon. Social services were there to assign him and his sister to foster care in the meantime. NO! He had exclaimed with some forcefulness. I am old enough to care for myself and my sister. We are not being split up and we are not going anywhere but home. The social service worker had looked at him with an attitude of great doubt, but she put her piece of paper away, again without his name on it. To his relief their grandmother had come and taken care of them and it hadn't really been left to him.

But, he had stood up again. Maybe it was something he could do. More importantly, however, the secret was out. His mother must be off her addiction before she would be released. There would be one less secret to keep. He had his others, deeper and darker than his mother, but one down was a success.

It was the third sheet that had brought him on his trip today. That sheet had already made a profound difference in his daily life and portended more for the future. That sheet had removed him from the shadows. No more had the teachers used him as the verbal whipping boy for the class. No more had other students regarded him with contempt. One simple sheet of paper, fully objective and without any bias had changed others' perception of him.

The loud speaker in the hallway had blared his name and summoned him immediately to the office. It was not the first time he had been called upon, but he could think of no cause for this one. The principal had risen when he entered the office and greeted him with a smile. It was obvious that no one had died. Then he was presented with the paper. It stated simply that he was, by objective fact, an honor scholar. He had received the highest score in the school and was in the top 5 in the county on a national test. His seating assignments in class had been rearranged closer to the front. Teachers who had mocked him now called him "mister" without scorn in their voice. In group activities others looked to him for answers. College, which had never even been in his plans, was now paid for. He could go on and learn to write!

But all these changes had not changed everything. They had not changed him. He had become academically accepted, but neither his social status nor his social skills had changed. Outside of class "alone" remained his domain.

And now, as the miles rolled past and his mother chatted amiably, he was on his way. He was on his way, though, with a secret, a secret so deep that no one knew. It was a secret that no one could know. His mind flashed back to the Reverend Stout. Yes, the devil had him by the nose and by the toes and was leading him inexorably to his doom. In all the elation and all the adulation, the sadness had not been erased. When he walked along the sidewalk that directly abutted the busy highway near his house he still gazed with a certain fascination at the big semis that sped along toward him. One simple step, he would tell himself over and over again, one simple step and it is done. He would recoil at the thought but then quickly return to it again.

Then there was the fear. Everyone is afraid of change, he had been reassured. But they didn't know the fear. It wasn't a fear that felt reassured. He looked at the blank sheet of paper in front of him, the blank sheet of his unwritten life, and trembled. Two simple words, I can't, echoed and reverberated in his brain. I can't go away. I can't leave home. I can't meet new people. I can't be alone again. I CAN'T BE ALONE AGAIN! As they drove into the town where the college was located, his heart did not flutter with anticipation; it shook with anxiety.

"Listen," the voice of the teacher was stern. "Your writing is hollow. It's empty. You are missing the element of the inner man. Release it. Release it. How you say? Drugs would be helpful. It will give you the perspective of true creativity. We haven't been reading Carlos Constaneda just to pass the time. Get out of your provincial mentality and join the world. You want to write? You can write, but you need that extra reality. Get some real inspiration!"

The young man trudged back to the dorm. He had made no friends. There was no one to talk to. He had had one flirtation that had ended in unequivocal rejection. He had not been the star pupil, the big fish in the small pond of high school. His new classmates had also scored in the top 10 percent nationally on tests. They had taken college prep classes his small school had not offered. Every day for seven months he had faced his own glaring inadequacies with increased pain and sorrow. He had been to the school counselor and been told to simply pull himself together. "This too shall pass, so don't worry about it, be happy" was their mantra. A broken heart, no friends and despair were not on their to-do list. And despair had set in as bleak and heartless as a cold February day. He had no desire or energy to do his school work and was failing. He had no desire to take care of his person and had become a repugnant mockery of his former self. But it was the late '60's and his new appearance aligned with that of thirty percent of all males on campus, so it too went unnoticed. Each thought of failure captured his mind as he plodded along alone.

Suddenly he knew he was not alone. "You see, young man," Reverend Stout spoke with firm conviction. "He's got you by the nose and he's got you by the toes and you are already halfway to hell."

"Reverend Stout, be damned," shouted the young man toward nothing at all. "Maybe you are wrong. Maybe the Reverend Peters who told me that God is dead is right. Either way there is no heaven and maybe there is no hell either. If there is one, though, I'm already in it, so shut up!" With a wry smile the Reverend Stout faded away. The young man found and paid his supplier for a fifth of cheap wine and sank into an unhappy oblivion.

When he awoke he considered the three options he saw open to him. Kill myself. Kill myself. Kill myself. Through bleary eyes he looked at the calendar. It was Good Friday. Maybe, he thought, I will go to church first. Reverend Stout is long dead. Reverend Peters has not helped; but maybe I will just go to church first. He showered and changed and wandered off campus to go wherever might present itself. It would be his last goodbye to God.

Three cars were parked outside a small church on a quiet side street. He cautiously peered in the door and saw a few worshippers spread around the nearly empty sanctuary. To his right was a stairway and he took it. From the empty balcony he looked down and watched the face of one elderly woman near the front. He watched her as if they were the only two people present. He didn't hear the priest. He didn't hear the music. It was just the two of them separated but together. She was all alone, but she didn't seem to be. Her face was full of a peace that he wanted to reach out and grab for himself. In quietness and contentment she sat and worshipped. As the service neared its end he slipped out before anyone noticed him and walked quietly back to campus. The following Monday he packed his bags, withdrew from all classes and left the school.

Depressed, but no longer seeing only three options, he walked down the street to the highway to hitch a ride to anywhere – anywhere but there. Again he felt a presence beside him. Turning he confronted the Reverend Stout. "I thought you had left," he said.

"Boy, I am not leaving. But you have another chapter to write. Daniel needs your help. Take that blank sheet and make something of it."

Chapter 4
The Prairie

Daniel took one last look at the Missouri as they crested the first hill and moved west. There is something eternal about rivers, he thought. Then looking ahead he saw the vast expanse of prairie under the brilliant blue dome of the sky. That too was endless, vast and endless. A sudden fear gripped him, a fear so real and present that he spun around seeking its source. But there was nothing but the creaking of wagons, the laughter of children and men yelling at their teams of horses and oxen. Daniel looked around again, carefully searching in every direction, but no threat appeared. His mind drifted back to an old man who had teased him the day before. "Goin' west, Sonny? Be careful you don't get yourself trampled by no herd o' buffalo." The old man had then spit a stream of tobacco juice into the nearest pot and laughed heartily. But that recollection brought him no fear. But still the sense of panic had not left.

The early May sun was warm and Daniel peeled off his outer coat. He knew that he could certainly walk faster than the pace of the lumbering oxen. Still, everyone had been warned not to move on too far ahead or wander off and expect to catch up. With his physical location restricted he let his thoughts wander instead. They roamed to a dark corner of his mind and turned to the strange malady that afflicted Miss Sally. She was never gay although she might brighten for a moment at some special sight or word. Some mornings he had seen that Tom was actually combing her hair for her. If other women gathered to talk she would remain silent or only occasionally insert a word or two. Mostly, though, she seemed to wander from the ongoing chatter of the circle and be somewhere else in her thoughts.

Daniel felt an affinity with her. He remembered with a twinge of sorrow how he had always been on the side and never in the middle of human activity. He had listened but not spoken, watched but not participated and had sat in the shade completely sapped of energy after having done nothing at all. These past weeks had brought a different response from him, but always he had seemed to be looking in on himself doing the things he was doing and not be the one doing them. A chill ran down his spine. Was he in the demon already and just watching his body go through the motions of life? Was he already separated from his life and watching the demon live it through him? If the devil already had him by the nose and toes as the Reverend Stout had said, was he really living his life or was his life being lived in?

He shook off the utter nonsense of the last question and returned to thoughts of Miss Sally. She was always sweet to him. She saved her few smiles mostly for Tom, but on an occasion or two had shared one with him. Miss Sally even talked to him a few times. The softness of her voice always entranced him. It was as if the gentleness of the sound pulled him right into her heart and welcomed him there. He hoped with all his heart that the trip would make her better. He wanted to pray but was afraid of God's wrath breaking out against the demon within him.

One evening, while still in Missouri, he had been carrying the water pail past a group of women. They were speaking in subdued voices but the still night air had carried their words straight to him. Summed up their combined conversation had been:

"Poor Tom, having to do everything by himself. That wife of his making excuses of some "strange disease". Pshaw! Just an excuse for laziness if you ask me."

"More likely," another had retorted, "sin, sin and the devil. The good book says they's demons. They got 'em then and still do, that's what I say."

Replied another hushed voice, "Needs to pray through is what she needs."

"Too far gone to pray as I hear it," concluded the comments Daniel had overheard before hurrying away from the scathing gossip.

Too far gone to pray, Daniel echoed in his mind as he brought his thoughts back to the present. But if I can't pray she gets better, will hoping get it done? In frustration he kicked the head off a low lying prairie flower. Anyway, his mind growled in anger, what do those old cats know? Miss Sally is a good person. I see her reading the good book every day. There has to be something else. There just has to be.

A week rolled by and the weather grew warmer each day and the trail grew a little less exciting. Miss Sally would ride beside Tom for a while after breakfast but then went into the wagon to lie down. Again in the early afternoon she would ride with him but never for long periods.

One evening after they had come to an early stop Tom surprised Daniel. "Son, would you like to learn how to drive the team? I get mighty sore sitting up there day after day. I could sure use some walking time if you could learn to handle the horses." Daniel knew how to hitch the horses but his Pa had never let him run the team. Too excited to speak he nodded his assent.

For the next two hours, while Miss Sally sat in the shade of another wagon, Tom drilled Daniel in the skills of wagon driving and team management. Seeing that Daniel's untrained arms were starting to fail, Tom ended the training for the day, but each afternoon he continued the lessons until they reached and crossed the Kansas River. The first day after the crossing Tom told Daniel to hitch the wagon and that he was the teamster for the day. Daniel nearly burst. He had been given real responsibility but even more, maybe Miss Sally would sit next to him and they could talk. He knew he could work the reins and talk at the same time. He needed to talk.

After the breakfast fires had all been extinguished the convoy of wagons set out. Daniel sat proudly on the seat and brought his wagon in line with the others. Before they moved again, Miss Sally climbed from the back and took her seat beside him. Daniel looked at her with sudden apprehension. Would this be Billy Logan all over again, all the words prepared and never said? In the privacy of just the two of them could he find his voice?

Miss Sally smiled, a weak smile, but to Daniel a smile never-the-less. When Daniel only smiled back she asked, "Cat got your tongue this morning, Daniel?"

The spell was broken. Billy Logan had never made the first move, but now Miss Sally had. They chatted amiably as the sun grew larger in the sky. Still the idle chatter had not come near the point that Daniel had to know. When he saw his companion start to stir a little he could contain himself no more. It was plunge in now or regret forever.

"Miss Sally," his voice cracked and grew silent. She cast expectant eyes on his. He started again but made only a croaking sound. Miss Sally reached out a frail hand and laid it on his arm. Again he tried and found his voice weak but working. "Can you tell me about melancholia?"

Her eyes rested gently on his face. "Such a strange question," she answered. "Do you really want to know or have all the chattering ladies piqued your curiosity?"

Daniel stammered his answer. "No, I really want to know. Those old cats say too much." His bluntness had startled him and he blushed deeply hoping it had not offended Miss Sally. He hoped she didn't think that was an admission that he was part of the gossip.

She pressed her fingers lightly into his arm, started to smile and then sighed. "It wasn't always like this Daniel. When Tom and I were courting we would go to dances and parties. But gradually I stopped having fun. Even before," and she choked a moment, "even before we lost our babies I had grown so tired. Every day was a chore to get up. Every good and right thing I wanted to do for Tom was a hard chore to do. I would drive myself to smile and be gay, to work on the farm and in the house, to gossip with the ladies at church socials, but I just always grew more tired, more sad, more, how shall I put it, disconnected with others. I still love Tom with all my heart and it makes me even sadder that I cannot seem to show it. I know what they say about me and about him. This I know Daniel, and I know it for sure, I believe in God the Father Almighty and in Jesus Christ His only Son our Lord." She stopped and sighed. "I really do. Now I have to rest." Slowly she maneuvered to the back of the wagon. Tears burned Daniel's eyes and he hoped he wouldn't steer the team into someone or something before he regained his sight.

The next three days they encountered a steady downpour. The ground grew soft and the progress slow. For three days Miss Sally did not appear outside the wagon. On the fourth day the sun again claimed the sky and Daniel again took the reins. Miss Sally again did not appear. From under the canvas top Daniel could hear murmurs mixed with an ever increasing cough. At noon he told Tom that something was wrong with Miss Sally. Two other women were called to ride with her and bring her what comfort they could. When the train stopped that night Miss Sally's cough had turned to a deep choking sound that Daniel could not stand to hear. Tom sent Daniel to another wagon for supper and when Daniel came back he found Tom sitting on the wagon seat sobbing heavy dry sobs.

Wagon trains don't stop. Life goes on and graves are left behind. Everyone knew the rules and everyone knew that it wouldn't happen to them, but they all hoped for the other's sake that they would find the strength to go on. The ground was still soft enough from the rain and the men still fresh enough from only a few weeks on the trail that they were able to dig a decent grave for Sally Miller. The captain of the train spoke a few words over the grave then put his arm around Tom and led him away. For a moment at least, Daniel was forgotten. He stood by the grave and when everyone had left he fell upon it and wept.

He lay upon it all night and the next morning when the teams were being hitched he did not move. Tom tried to pull him to his feet but he resisted. The captain of the train tried to lift him from the ground but Daniel fought back vigorously. In the end with all pleas and entreaties fallen on deaf ears, the train moved out. Tom left Daniel a blanket and another family left him a jug of water and loaf of bread. They all assured him that another train would be along in a few days and that they could all catch up at Fort Laramie.

Oblivious to their kind words Daniel had lain face down in the new sod atop the grave and gave no one a response. Slowly the sound of lowing oxen, laughing children, creaking axles and plodding horses faded into the sounds of birds and insects. The sun rose, burned hot and set and Daniel lay bereft in heart and exhausted with crying. The moon rose on the tranquil prairie and the scurrying sounds of small animals could be heard in the tall grass.

Gradually Daniel could feel the earth beneath him start to tremble. The other night sounds began to subside. The earth shook more and a dull throbbing sound became evident. Daniel sat up and looked across the moonlit bathed prairie. Something was there, but it was too far to see. The earth began to rock and the violence of its shaking brought Daniel springing to his feet. The throbbing had become a thunderous roar. Now under the bathing light of the full moon he could see and for a moment his heart trembled like the earth. Then in peace he laid back down on Miss Sally's grave. The herd of stampeding buffalo was pounding ever closer. Daniel embraced the grave and waited.

Chapter 5
Interlude (Soft Music Plays)

Hand trembling and heart pounding the young man laid his pen down on the desk. With unseeing eyes he stared at the chalkboard. He seemed to have failed in his assigned task from the Reverend Stout. Failed miserably in fact.

The buzzing of a hive of bumble bees ran through his right ear. Distractedly he shook his head to rid it of the sound and saw Dr. Connealy standing beside him. Suddenly he was aware that the buzzing had been words, but words unheard by his wandering mind.

"Sorry, sir. What did you say?"

"If my grandmother were standing here she would ask, 'picking wool'?"

"Uh, no. I seem to have written myself into an impasse." The young man replied and placed his hand over the sheet he had been writing on.

"I would say it looks more like you have written yourself into a state of shock. Is it because your writing is so good that it is shocking? Good writers sometimes lay out things in such a way that it even shocks them. You are a good writer. I hope I have made that clear. Now, were you going someplace with your story and got lost?"

"No. Well, I mean, I was going someplace with the story, yes. I don't think I got lost. I just got to an impasse."

"Obviously your hand tells me you don't want me to see it at the present time."

The young man blushed but he didn't move his hand. "Can I just say it's complicated?"

"You can, but it is a phrase without meaning and I would edit it on your paper. Can you rescue your train of thought from your impasse?"

"That may be difficult. I just killed my main character."

"Is he dead dead, or just pretend dead? Lots of main characters seem to die, but we find that they really haven't as we read on." The young man felt the panic that Daniel had felt back at the Missouri. His face paled and his body twitched involuntarily. His mind raced for a reason for his sudden sensation. "Are you alright?" the professor asked with concern.

Swallowing hard and taking a deep breath the young man replied, "Um. Yeah. Yeah. Sure." Not feeling the least bit sure he hoped the bell would soon ring.

"Do you have a class next hour?" Dr Connealy asked.

"No."

"Neither do I. This room will be empty. Stick around and we will try to unwind your impasse." The professor continued to circle the room, commenting and assisting each student as needed. The young man removed his hand from the paper and stared at his last sentence.

The room cleared quickly after the bell and Dr. Connealy closed the door to offer a quieter and more private interview. "So how did your hero die?"

"Trampled in a buffalo stampede."

"That is certainly a new method and certainly more permanent than falling off a bridge."

"Yes, but he can't die."

"But it appears that he has. Unless, of course, a lightning bolt should smash into the earth right in front of the lead buffalo and divert the path of the herd."

"That would work, I guess. Kind of corny, don't you think?"

"Yes, it is. He could maybe run as fast as he could and hide behind a very big rock."

"No, he can't. He is stuck where he is. It would be out of character for him to move."

"Then he's dead."

"He can't be dead. If he dies, I am dead."

"Art and reality sometimes collide, but you wouldn't really be dead. If you erased the sentence would you be erasing him?"

"I can't erase him. I can't erase the buffalo. I can't erase me. The whole book has built to this point. The buffalo stampede has to take place. He has to be trampled. He has to live. I can't explain it. It's . . . it's . . . it's just that that has been the focus of the book. It has been the necessary outcome from the beginning."

"So this isn't just a short story for my class. It could stand as a short story, but it is really part of a greater whole. Is that right?"

"The character and I have been together for more than five years. I had to write this chapter to help him out. Reverend Stout said so." And now he had said too much and he knew it, but Dr. Connealy did nothing more than raise his eyebrows a little. His voice remained the same calm and understanding voice it had been as he replied.

"And who is the Reverend Stout?" There was really no way out of answering and Dr. Connealy looked like he would really like an answer and maybe even try to understand one.

"He's a character in the book."

"So he's been with you for the past five years as well." It wasn't a question and it wasn't said with cutting sarcasm.

"Yes. You see he had sort of condemned Daniel. That's the character's name. But then last year right after Easter he told me Daniel was in trouble and I needed to write the next chapter. That sounds really crazy doesn't it? I mean really crazy."

"What were you doing last Easter?" The simplicity and sincerity of the question propelled the young man to divulge more than he had ever intended.

"Getting ready to quit school. I had gone to another college and I just didn't make it. I felt alone and lost and every day I felt more alone and lost. I didn't have my Daniel story out all year. Anyway, I went to a small church on Good Friday and when I came out of it I knew I had to leave school. I hitchhiked around a little but within two weeks I was home. Then all the alone just washed off me like dirt under a strong shower. My mom had moved and now she lives just up the road from here. I felt like I could do it here. The state said I could have one more chance and gave me back my scholarship. I have a girlfriend and I'm happy."

"So when did Reverend Stout tell you to write the chapter?"

"Oh, yeah. Well, when I was leaving campus he sort of came up beside me and told me to write a chapter because Daniel needed my help."

"And you have waited until now to do it?"

"I don't know why. It is just that, well, I guess, I have been feeling a little like Daniel lately."

"How's that?"

"Kind of like getting stepped on by a buffalo."

"Not a whole herd, just one? But Daniel got trampled by a herd."

"I can't really have one lone buffalo wandering across the prairie and accidently stepping on him, can I?" He felt relieved at the humor he could see in that picture.

"You are a great writer. You really are. Probably the best in my class for the past many years. You will write captivating novels someday. Beware of being sucked into them. It happens. I'm sure you can find the right exit from your impasse. You know where you want your character to end up and what else needs to happen to him. Since you know where you are going I trust you will find your way to get there. Keep writing. Your novels will do well."

Unexpectedly, especially to himself, the young man burst out, "But I want to write poetry."

Dr. Connealy, who had half risen, sat down again. "Poetry, huh. Well, that is a very difficult field. It is very subjective. Do you have a preferred style?"

"I am really rather locked into a style that is rhythmic. The stanzas have a nice consistent meter that is easy to follow. I feel really comfortable writing with a meter of 8-6 or 8-7 or 8-8. It is not hard for me to make those patterns into meaningful rhymes."

"Do you go to church?" The question was shocking. Could a demon even get inside one he wondered? He guessed that it had last Good Friday.

Without thinking it through he answered. "Reverend Stout says it's not likely to help me. I did go as a child."

"Did he tell that to you or Daniel?"

"Well, I guess it was to Daniel. Why do you ask if I go to church?"

"The strict meter of your poetry is the meter of a whole lot of good church music." Receiving no response he continued. "My job is that of a professor and not that of a counselor or pastor. I do think, however, that your friend Daniel needs a second opinion to that of Reverend Stout. I also think you should concentrate on finishing this chapter for your short story assignment and then devote some real time to it as a book. Your writing is clear and obviously it creates a real environment for the reader. Just don't get caught in that place. You live here. And please, see if you can't get Daniel a second opinion. Now you have to keep him alive." With that he stood and the young man knew he had been dismissed.

"Thank you. Thank you very much." And smiling he walked out the door.

Chapter 6
Memories

Dawn spread its golden fingers across the prairie. The cry of the coyote and the screech of the owl became still while the trill of the red-winged blackbird greeted the sun. Warblers and buntings competed in calling for their mates. Killdeer echoed a refrain.

Slowly the busy cries of morning penetrated Daniel's mind. The sun was pleasant but not hot. A May chill still refreshed the day. Daniel opened his eyes and closed them again in a state of confusion. Hell couldn't be this pleasant, he thought, and I have heard in heaven there is no pain. Indeed a night of lying face down on cold hard earth had left him in great discomfort. His legs and arms and neck were stiff. I feel like I've been run over by a herd of buffalo, he thought.

Pushing himself up with a start he looked around. That was it. He had been stampeded by a herd of buffalo. He had seen them clearly in the bright moonlight. He should be dead and felt mostly as if he were. Daniel examined his clothes and they were not torn. He examined his hands and they were not scratched or broken. The prairie around him was unmolested by the hooves of a million buffalo. It wasn't a dream, he assured himself. They were there. I saw them. I felt the earth shake and the roaring of their stampede nearly deafened me. But there is no sign of them.

Beside him still lay the jug of water and paper wrapped loaf of bread. He unwrapped the bread and brushed off the insects that had dined there already. Slightly refreshed by food and drink he walked with a stiff and stumbling gait toward the last spot he had seen the herd. It wasn't more than two hundred yards, he knew it wasn't, but there were still no signs of any buffalo having been there. He walked on and kept searching, always with the same result. "Getting lost on the prairie is an easy thing to do, son," he remembered the wagon master saying. He dared not go too far. Turning he could again see the cross atop Miss Sally's grave. It was small and now nearly hidden from view by the tall grass nearer to him. The grave, at least, was real. Sorrow gripped his heart but his eyes were drained of tears.

His muscles now stretched a little from the walk he began to run back to the cross as a beacon in a wide and empty land. The grave was only a few yards off the trail. He had to stay there. New wagon trains were heading out every few days from Independence and another one would be here. For now, though, he was alone. Never had he felt so alone. There had always been someone to watch, but alone was different than just being on the outside looking in.

A thought flashed in his mind. But I'm not alone. I can talk to Miss Sally until someone else comes. I can tell her all the things I've wanted to tell somebody all my life. He was certain that she had understood him and the pain he felt during their brief talk on the wagon although he had said nothing to her about it. He was equally certain that she would help him now with her silent questions to draw out his thoughts into words. Daniel sat once again on her grave but as he tried to begin his lips trembled, his voice would not come and he was quickly wracked with dry sobs. Sitting on her grave, arms wrapped around his legs, face buried in his knees he rocked slowly back and forth waiting for the strength to talk to come.

"I'm not lazy, Miss Sally," he began. "It's just that there are days I can't seem to get going. My body is sore and tired and I haven't done anything except lie in my bed. Yes, I know you know. I've seen you, Miss Sally, try to brush your hair and you just couldn't do it. I saw the tears fill your eyes as Tom took the brush and helped you.

"I couldn't cry, though, Miss Sally. Pa would shout at me, 'Quit yore bawlin', boy" and then whack me so hard I had to cry anyway. He never said to me 'What's the matter?' He never touched me softly like I saw Tom touching you. He'd just yell some more and say, 'The devil's in you, boy, and it's my God ordained responsibility to drive him out. Now git out to that field and hoe them corn rows. If you want to eat you gotta work. Work will drive the laziness out o' you'."

Daniel sighed with the remembrance. Then plucking a stem of grass and putting it in his mouth he continued. "I know, Miss Sally, that the other kids at school talked behind my back like those old cats talked behind yours. 'He's so stupid', the girls would say. 'He can't give any of the answers.' But I could, Miss Sally, I could. I knew them all. It's just that one time I tried to stand up and give them and I nearly fainted just like a girl. No offense, please, Miss Sally. My head swam and my eyes couldn't see the teacher and no words came from my mouth. But I knew all the answers. I did. And the boys would say, 'He can't play tag. He just turns in circles and doesn't chase anybody. He can't do anything.' And they were right, Miss Sally. I didn't chase anybody. I never knew who to pick. I would look around and around at all of them laughing and saying 'try and catch me' and then I just couldn't move."

A tear crept into the corner of his eye as he remembered the mockery of the other children. "But I wasn't just afraid at school, Miss Sally, I was afraid at church, too. All of us were told to memorize Psalm 23. Ma worked on it with me. I learned it in one morning. I knew it perfect. When we met with the Reverend Stout for Sunday school, well Sarah Barnes stood up in her brand new dress and flipped her braids back over her shoulders and went first. She didn't know it, Miss Sally. She got stumped after 'I shall not want'. Reverend Stout had to help her with all the rest. The next two didn't know it either, but they got farther than she did. Then when it was my turn I went up and nothing came out of my mouth. Nothing, Miss Sally. Nothing at all. Reverend Stout said, 'You lazy boy. The devil will keep you from learning His word and pretty soon he will just take you by the nose and take you by the toes and take you straight to the eternal pit of fire with him. I'm going to tell your Pa that you didn't learn this so that he can make sure you do get it learned.' Ma helped me, though. She told Pa that I knew every word and then held me by the hand while I gave it straight through. I still got a lickin', though, for having been too idle minded for not giving it to the Reverend."

Daniel paused. He started to speak again and then hesitated. Could he tell her the rest? Maybe, he thought, it would be enough to just tell her the sorrows and not the rest of the fears. Both were something he had never told to anyone. Miss Sally, though, would understand. At least she would understand the sorrows. He plunged on.

"Miss Sally, I ain't complaining about the lickin's. Every kid gets licked. Except, I don't think Sarah Barnes ever did. It was Pa's job to lick us and keep us right. But there was more, Miss Sally. There were the days when the sun would shine so bright and I would only see a gray sky. Ma would say, 'Look at the beautiful day.' She used to say that when I was little. But as I got older the beautiful days never made Ma smile any more. She would just start to cry for no reason and then I would start to cry too and then I had to run quick out to the barn before either she or Pa saw me crying. Days got grayer and darker, so dark I just wanted to sleep. Then Pa would yell, the sun's high in the sky, boy. Git to work. I would go to work, but I didn't see the sun. Then some days the sun was just there and I was happy to hoe the field. There was a man in the town near us. He was crazy. He acted crazy all the time and I thought I was going to be just like him. The other children laughed, Miss Sally, and I couldn't laugh. The other children would sing during music time and I would just put my head down and cry. The other children would play and I would imagine myself playing. I was going to be as crazy as the old man in town. The Reverend Stout said the devil already had him and now he was working on me."

Again Daniel stopped his narrative. He felt he had cut closer to the bone than he had ever thought he could go. Having gone so far, though, he hesitated to continue but also sensed he had to finish his story. He reached into the bundle of his clothes and pulled out his deepest secret.

"Do you see this, Miss Sally," he asked as he held up a well honed knife. "I sleep with it every night. I would wake up and see the devil climbing up the ladder to my loft and he would stop and stare at me with fiery eyes. He was a monster. I can't tell you how horrible he looked. He would reach for the top step of the ladder and shake a little like he was ready to leap off it and into my bed. One day I hoed weeds for the next farmer over and he gave me twenty-five cents. I didn't tell Pa. When we next went to town I went to the livery 'cause I knew a man there who had a nice knife. I asked him where I could get a knife like his and he sold me one for twenty-five cents. You can see it's nicked a little and had some rust, but I keep it honed. I slept with it every night and when the devil would come up the ladder I would take it out. I still sleep with it. But that isn't all. I look at it sometimes and think it would be easier if I just used it on myself and not just wait for the devil do all his work. I stroke the back of it over my wrists sometimes just to get the feel. Miss Klausmann over in Wabash did it for real. The Reverend Stout wouldn't even do her funeral. Cursed forever he said. The Klausmann's moved on after that. So I say to myself, Miss Sally, do I let the devil take me slow or do I just rush it along since I'm cursed forever anyway?"

Miss Sally's answer came in the creaking of a wagon axle and the snort of a horse. Daniel looked behind him and he wasn't alone anymore.

Chapter 7
Hope

The young man looked with aggravation at the engine heat gauge on his car. That, coupled with the unpleasant clanging from under the hood, did not bode well for his cash flow. Already he had three dates lined up for the week, and although one was only a lunch date, he could ill afford a major expense.

Life had been busy, had become a real whirlwind of living, during the year since his private visit with and encouragement from Dr. Connealy. Being at home had stabilized his emotions for the most part. It had given him an impetus to break into a new persona. He had been feted along with four other college students as the up and coming new leadership for his community. His engagement to his previous girlfriend having failed he had rebounded with an astounding social life with its own little black book. Grades which had struggled to meet with success two years earlier had become top of the class. A satisfactory job, activities with others, volunteer activity in the community and even actively attending church had filled out his life. But he had also abandoned his pen and portfolio. He had buried them in a place where he hoped to hide his darkness and live a brand new life.

It was, in fact, a perfect life to look in upon. That was the young man's own assessment. It wasn't real, of course. It wasn't him, but it was a more satisfying veneer than what he had lived in the past. Life was motion without emotion, a façade without an interior. It was mere busyness for busyness sake. The question each day was simply, how long can this fakery last? Was this all he ever had to look forward to? No! That thought couldn't exist. It always had to be dismissed. It was this or the darkness, the pit which even home could not fully lighten. Which darkness, he often wondered, motion without emotion or inner demons too dark to fight, would be the better life? Maybe neither, but that was too dark a corner to look into.

Looking again at the soaring heat gauge and hearing the persistent knocking, he pulled into the service station near his home. "It's the water pump, young man. It will be sixty dollars and I can fix it tomorrow."

That was certain to curtail the veneer for a while; the while beginning after his already planned engagements. Good thing, he thought, I have already paid for the tickets for my date with Chris. There should be enough left over, if we eat light, to buy tickets to the movie premier with Erin on Saturday as well. It was going to knock out bowling with the guys that week, but that was an easier sacrifice to make.

While he and the mechanic stood looking under the hood of his car, another visitor had entered the garage. Looking up the young man froze. Standing in the door was his greatest fear from high school. The bully, his own personal bully, the every night I am going to pound you into the earth bully, was standing there. Their eyes locked. The bully looked down at the side of the door in which he stood and saw a piece of iron pipe. Picking it up he approached the young man while pounding one end of the pipe repeatedly into his other open hand.

Surprisingly the pipe did not take a swing in the young man's direction. Surprisingly the bully put out his hand in a gesture of friendship and warmly said, "Hi. How've you been?"

The mechanic disappeared. The car disappeared. The entire garage disappeared. All that existed was the young man, the bully and the radio in the background. The radio had to stay; the music had to play. It was a current hit transforming the confrontation from the past to the present. "Uh, hi," the young man breathed out the words slowly. Realizing that he still had life and breath and a totally uninjured body he stammered out the very first words that raced in his mind. "Bob, you've changed." The bully looked at him and the young man assessed that those might not have been the best words to speak.

"Yeah, I have." Stop the music, commercial break, bad timing for sure; wait for the explosion. "I've been in the Navy. While I was on ship someone told me about Jesus. I received Him as my Savior. Yeah, I've changed."

Time warp voice over to give clarity to the moment. As the words "someone told me about Jesus" were being spoken, the commercial on the radio began announcing a "Meet Jesus" rally with an upbeat Christian band was going to be held in a nearby city. As the final words, "I've changed" were being said, before there was another word spoken, the commercial told when and where the rally would be held.

Re-entering real time the young man said, "Oh. That's nice." Then Bob also disappeared as the young man thought, that's tonight. I can't go. I don't have a car. Then to Bob who had reappeared he said, "So, what else has been happening in your life?"

"Got married. We live out in San Diego right now. Just came home for a few days. Had to stop in and buy some gas. Gotta go. Good seeing you again." Then Bob really did disappear, the mechanic was back; the garage was back and the radio played on while no one listened. Assured his car would be ready tomorrow at one, the young man also disappeared.

As he walked the few blocks back to his home the young man rehearsed the words of the commercial over and over. They became a tape on an endless reel. Why, he wondered. What was so magnetic about them? Anyway, he remembered with a jolt, I have class tonight. I couldn't have gone anyway. Better get home and see if I can borrow Mom's car.

Like the song that never ends, it became the commercial without end. As he drove to class that night there it was again. This time, alone and undistracted, he heard it all. The rally wasn't just tonight; it was tonight and tomorrow night both. No date; no plans; no obstacles were left. But where was this place? There was an obstacle. It was in a part of a nearby city where he had never been. There was a test on Friday and he planned to keep his "A" average going. There was another obstacle. Totally distracted he parked the car and went in to his math class. Statistical analysis, however, could not captivate his mind. The commercial kept running while more obstacles arose to shut it out. What, he wondered, are the statistical probabilities that I will not pass this test if I don't start to pay attention? Still arguing with himself he was glad for the bell and drove home, again hearing the commercial.

Work was a blur; classes were a blur; friends were a blur; plans for the weekend were a blur. Hour after hour the confrontation was coming. Obstacles, ever increasing obstacles, versus the never ending commercial, which was now only playing in his mind, was the supreme contest of the day. What had the commercial insinuated but not actually said? What was it insinuating into his mind every time it ran? Meet a friend like no other. That was it. That was what ran between the lines over and over again.

He thought of the friends he now ran with. Was it as much a false pose to them as to him? Were they all fleeing a stark darkness within by showing a poster boy front without? Did they fear the gripping sense of isolation if friends faded away? Did they see themselves in the masquerade or was it only him? It had been a topic never shared or discussed. The whole concept seemed to him to be total foreignness to them. They had never seemed to live in his darkness. They had all lived daily while he had died daily. No, the façade was crumbling and he knew it. No, he couldn't live an entire life as a painted empty shell. What was it again that had been implied? Yes. Meet a friend like no other.

Like a magnet the commercial directed his car down the rain darkened side street to the gymnasium where the rally would be held. Like a magnet it drug his feet from the car and up to the gym door. It was packed. All the old fears returned. It was packed. It wasn't packed with people he knew. He was in a strange place with strangers. He trembled. The car was only a few steps away. He was leaving everything all over again. He was in a place that wasn't home, that wasn't even part of the false front that he had created for his own safety. It was a place set apart and he had learned to avoid places set apart. Still he entered and then stood with a second wave of fear as he looked at the new place, the new people but with the old uncertainty.

Ignoring contact he made his way to the last row of bleachers. There it wasn't crowded. He sat down and rested his back against the gym wall. The music began and it was good. Some, many of the people sang along. He didn't know any of the songs but was pleased to hear them. Then the music from the band stopped but began again with the speaker. He was young, not much older than the one who sat alone in the back of the gym. The words of "Killing Me Softly with His Song" sang along in the young man's mind with each word he heard being spoken.

The room was diminished to just the two of them. How could this young speaker know the young man so well? How could he tell his life with such complete accuracy? How could he expose the pain and hurt that existed so deeply? How could he have read each word the young man had written and now sing them out loud for everyone to hear? How could he know him and his despair? How could this stranger see inside him, through him, and tell his whole story? But beyond the story there was a simple proclamation: there was a friend who would forgive and forget the past and move ever onwards in love. The young man burned as he heard the words. It began as an agony but became a funeral pyre for his life of hopelessness and despair. It became a fire of warmth and home. So the young man sat, transfixed, unmoving when so many others moved to the front at the end of the message. He had already moved, moved in his soul. But he did not yet know that he had also moved into the sights of the chief of all demons who would target his physical ills with a renewed and more vigorous spiritual attack.

Chapter 8
Headed Up or Down

They had gathered in the living room, a group of young adults in search of God's truth for their lives. Each of them, like the young man coming of age, had found their Friend in Jesus during or in the wake of the Meet Jesus Rally. They lounged in chairs or on the sofa or lay on the floor. The Bible study had been going well or at least as well as a group of young believers could do without trained leadership. Mostly it had been reading the Scriptures and sharing opinions which, at best, were mostly uninformed opinions. Still everyone in the group was eager to meet and read and pray. Questions were asked and a diligent search of the Bible was made to try and find an answer. Since few knew where to look, however, the answers were received as probabilities and not necessarily certain truth.

On the sofa sat a young girl with waist length brown hair. New people were always welcome in the group and she was one. She had been contributing her share of both questions and answers. Each night their leader was whoever happened to be host and as he felt things were winding down he asked if there were any other things they wanted to discuss. Speaking up the young girl said, "What about suicide?" Everyone eagerly grabbed their Bibles to find an answer but were held up by the leader who asked the girl to clarify her issue. "Well," she answered, "I really have two questions. "Can a person who is a Christian commit suicide and if a person does commit suicide would they go to heaven or hell?"

"You're not contemplating anything in particular, are you?" the leader joshed and the girl laughed and shook her head.

"No. It is just something I heard once as a kid and I was just wondering. A lot of people seem to do it. Maybe I phrased the question wrongly. I guess the first question is - is suicide a sin? Is it a different kind of sin than other sins? I don't know where to start the question so we can just pick any of those questions and go with it." She smiled and looked eagerly around the room.

"Well, suicide would be like murder, wouldn't it?" offered the first responder. "Do murderers go to heaven?"

"David murdered Bathsheba's husband and Paul murdered Christians," contributed another. "Aren't they going to be in heaven?"

"Yes, of course," chimed in another. "But they all repented afterwards."

The first responder jumped back in. "And the person who kills themselves can't do that."

Heads were nodded as Bible pages were turned to see if there was another answer. "What about Judas," asked another member of the group? "He committed suicide. Jesus said it was better if he hadn't even been born."

"Yeah, but that's not the reason why," the girl with the long brown hair contributed. "He was condemned for betraying Jesus."

"Yeah," the Judas contributor replied, "that's true."

Another girl leaning on her boyfriend's arm asked, "Wouldn't committing suicide be like saying you have no faith in God's ability to help you? Isn't that kind of like betraying Him?"

"I don't know about betraying Him," her boyfriend replied, "but it would seem to be a real lack of faith. Maybe that just showed that he didn't have faith in the first place so he was never a Christian."

"That's a real possibility," three people responded at once.

A lull came in the rush of questions and answers. The leader turned to the young man coming of age who was sitting quietly on the floor with his back propped against the side of an overstuffed chair. "What do you think? You haven't given us your ideas yet. Usually you have something to say and usually it's helpful. Contribute, Great Sage."

The young man looked around the room. Why, he thought, have they decided to discuss this question? Why look at me? If they knew where I have been with these thoughts they would probably never trust my answers again. As he scanned the room he could clearly see that all eyes were firmly fixed on him. He struggled in his mind for an answer. The answer of the Reverend Stout flashed in his mind. "She can't have a Christian burial. She's cursed forever." He shook that answer off and focused on the group. All their answers, though, had been a lot like Reverend Stout's answers, though they were phrased a little differently. But Reverend Stout had also said that people like Miss Sally had been taken by the devil and Miss Sally was certain that she believed in Jesus. That was her true hope.

"Come on," the host urged. "Quit stalling."

"I think this question might be above my pay grade," the young man chuckled. "Different groups have come to different conclusions. I'm not sure we can settle it tonight." Of course it wasn't a satisfactory answer as the response quickly showed.

"Well, one of those conclusions must be right, mustn't it? The Bible has an answer for everything. Quit stalling and give us your two cents worth," countered a girl from the far side of the room. Her comment received a chorus of assent from the others.

"Come on smarty pants," the host continued. "You're the one heading off to become a preacher. Somebody's gonna ask you that question some day and they'll want a better response than the one you just gave." Heads nodded in agreement.

"All right," the young man slowly began his response. "There are four questions right now on the floor. Which one begs the first answer?"

They all looked at the girl who had posed the question at the beginning. "Well, let's see," she said. "First would be – is suicide a sin?"

"Yes," the young man replied. "As someone said earlier it shows lack of faith. Paul said, in Romans I think, 'whatever is not from faith is sin'. That would be true of many things that we do every day. We worry. That is not from faith. We have pride. That is not from faith. Pretty much all sin reflects a lack of faith at the moment it is done."

The others looked at him with silent nods but added no comments so he continued, "What was the second question?"

The girl was ready. "Is suicide a worse sin than others?"

"I think it's in James 2 but we should look it up." The group turned there and each read it silently. "Is there a category of greater and lesser sins or are they all the same?" he asked.

"It seems they are all the same," came the general answer from many.

"Then," the young man said, "the answer to question two is no. It is hard for us to always accept that, but it is still 'no'. So, what is question three?"

"Can a Christian commit suicide?" the girl quickly responded.

"Can a Christian rashly do anything that is sin?" he answered. "For example, we all want to keep ourselves pure until we are married, right?" He looked at the young couple sitting together and everyone laughed. The young couple slid slightly apart for a moment and nodded along with everyone in the group. "But," the young man continued, "couldn't too much time alone and one little kiss lead to something that wasn't intended at the outset? It was a response to a momentary impulse and then the deed was done. There is no turning back the clock on it. That situation would be an overt sin. Maybe we experience a rashful moment of murderous hatred at someone for what they did. Jesus taught in the Sermon on the Mount that murder in the heart is the same as murder in the act. Those sins are covert sins. Every moment of every day we rashly commit both overt and covert sins. Many we don't even think about and certainly don't take the time to confess. If every rash sin brought us to damnation we would never ever be sure we were saved. I think that answers both questions three and four."

The group grew silent. The word "but" began to form on many lips but was not uttered. "So you're saying," also ran through many minds but was likewise not said. A few nodded their heads in agreement. The young couple snuggled again. It was not the answer the young man had thought he would give. He was a little surprised himself at what had come out. Seeing the lack of broad acceptance to his comments he formed one concrete thought, I can never tell them who I really am or what I really think. Though his thoughts of such things had become far more remote, they were neither gone nor forgotten. Then the questions pounced on his back as they had so many times in the months since he met Christ. Can I really be a minister of the Gospel? Can I really give hope when inside there is sometimes no hope? If the truth ever came out would I ever be accepted again? Then the clinching accusation, the very questions raised by his friends, raked its claws across his mind. Am I really in Christ if I have these thoughts and questions?

As the group finished prayer and slowly went on their ways the young man again longed for one thing. Would he ever find someone he could talk to about his feelings? Could that someone really give him the answers that he was so ready to give to others? Would that someone continue to trust him as a viable candidate for ministry if he talked to them about these issues? He was very glad for the friends he had, real friends he felt, not like those who were just there when his life was a sham. These were real friends but how he felt seemed to provoke an uneasy response in them. If he ever told them his darkest thoughts he could certainly stay a part of the group but he would then be seen by them with pity and concern and never taken seriously again.

"I liked your answer." The words broke in upon his thoughts. Turning he came face to face with the young girl who had asked the questions. "I rode tonight with Tim and Sue, but they want to go out and eat and I have to get home because I work early tomorrow. Could I bum a ride from you?" Her green eyes flashed a quick smile and he found no grounds for disagreement.

After dropping her off the young man went home and began sorting through the things he would want or need to take with him to school in a few weeks. As he opened a box in his closet he came across the portfolio of his writing. Long time since I saw you, he thought. He sat down and scanned through some of the pages. Dr.

Connealy's comments were scattered across many of them. He listened well, thought the young man. Maybe I could stop by and talk to him. As that thought passed his mind he came upon the last page of his favorite manuscript. He'll probably ask me how Daniel is doing. I guess I better find out myself. He picked up a pen and sat down to write.

Chapter 9
Home

"Tom!" Daniel yelled as he bolted from the ground and raced toward the approaching wagon. Tom set the brake and climbed down to meet the rushing youth and give him a warm embrace. "You came back," panted Daniel still hugging his friend. "You came back." He buried his face in Tom's shoulder and shook with silent sobs.

Tom held him tightly until the young man's composure was regained. Then he held him at arm's length, looked fully at him and then embraced him again. "Yes, Daniel, I'm back." I couldn't very well go on without you, now could I?"

"But everyone else," Daniel stammered and looked up the trail.

"Everyone else is going on, Daniel. Trains don't stop. People do. You did and I was a fool to leave you." Tom led Daniel to the shady side of the wagon. "Come sit down, son, I need to talk to you." They sat in the grass that had already been warmed by the morning sun and Tom handed Daniel a canteen of water. Then taking a long drink himself he began.

"Daniel, I had never done much learning about Oregon. People said the west was nice and Sally needed to get away from Toledo. We hooked up with some others and took off without really knowing where we were going. We just knew we would go someplace better for Sally.

"All the while we were traveling I spent a lot of time taking care of Sally and never really got to visiting with the other people. That all changed as we went along yesterday. Folks knew I would need some company and so they got to talkin' to me. I learned a whole lot about Oregon that I didn't know. It wasn't going to be a good place for Sally. She didn't like the heat and she didn't like cloudy skies. Some of the folks on the train had got letters from friends in Oregon. Yes, it's a mighty fine place to grow crops. The winters aren't too cold, but the summers are awful hot. While the winters aren't too cold, this friend who had written said that if you were lucky in the winter you might get one sunny day out of five. Oh, I felt bad, Daniel. Here I was trying to get a sunny place for Sally and where was I taking her? A place with one sunny day out of five; how could I do that to her? Oh, Daniel, I should have been in less of a hurry." Then Tom's shoulders sagged and he put his face in his hands and cried.

Daniel sat quietly and listened to the hum of the insects in the grass and the calls of the birds sitting on the tall stems. He heard the peace around him and finally laid his hand on Tom's arm and said, "Tom, don't feel too bad. The trip made Miss Sally happy. She looked forward to it and it seems that God has given her a right sunny spot to stay." Then he rested his head on Tom's shoulder and their tears mingled together on the ground.

The peaceful noises of the prairie seeped with soothing warmth into their souls. Tom took the kerchief from his pocket and dried his eyes. "Well, Daniel, you are right. The thought of a better place made her happy. What do you say that we just spend a few days here with her and wait for the next train and see where it is heading?"

After a quick trail lunch Tom cleared his throat and began, "I have something else to talk with you about, Daniel. Sally kept a little journal and also some notes in her Bible. She wrote about the day you two talked while you were driving the wagon. She said you were kind and seemed to really understand how she felt. She said, Daniel, that she thought you had the same kinds of thoughts and feelings that she did. Is that true?"

Daniel looked away from Tom. He was afraid that if their eyes met he could not say what he had to say. "I think so, Tom. The Reverend Stout, from back in Wabash, said the devil had me. My Pa said the devil had me and he wouldn't keep feeding the devil's own until the day of perdition. I don't know if I know all about how Miss Sally felt, but I think I know enough to say that I feel a lot like that too."

"Well, Daniel," Sally thought you did and she was a smart woman. "She left a note in her journal for me. Last night I couldn't sleep so I read some of the last things she said. She wrote them in those last days when she was in the wagon. 'Tom,' she said, 'you have to take care of Daniel for me. I won't be here to do it myself. He knows me, Tom. He knows my heart and my mind.'

"If I'd' a known that before last night, Daniel, I don't know what I'd a done. But when I saw it and had already learned about Oregon, I knew what I had to do." He paused and looked around the wide expanse of prairie, breathed deeply of its fragrance, gazed at the clear blue and cloudless sky then continued. "Do you like the prairie, Daniel?"

Daniel lay back in the grass and looked at the same cloudless sky. "Oh, yes, Tom. It's beautiful." Then he sat up with a sudden thought that set his body trembling. "Only thing is though, there are a lot of buffalo."

Tom looked in every direction. "Daniel, I don't see any buffalo."

"Oh, Tom, last night they were here. There were a million of them pounding the ground until it shook like the end of the world."

Tom stood up and surveyed the regions all around where they were camped. "Daniel, I am no authority on many things, but I do know what a place would look like if a hundred head of cattle had gone pounding over it just last night. The ground would be torn up bad. The grass wouldn't have sprung back like this already. Are you sure you didn't just dream it?"

"I sure thought I was sure. When I woke up this morning I didn't know how I woke up. Was I in heaven or hell? I felt so sore that one was a real possibility, but then I looked around and saw the sunshine and flowers and heard the birds sing and thought maybe I was in the other place. I went looking all over for those tracks you can't see and I couldn't see them either. But last night there was this noise. It started slow and then built. The night sounds all got real quiet and then the earth started to tremble a little and then it started to shake like a steam engine ready to blow. I looked across the prairie right there," and he pointed to the northwest, "and there they were, the biggest herd of buffalo ever seen and they were coming right at me. For just a moment I was afraid but then I lay down on Miss Sally's grave and just waited in peace for the end."

"You know, Daniel, Sally was right about you. You are like her and you know her well. That makes you extra special to me. We lived near the west end of Lake Erie. That lake can be just as beautiful a sight as you can imagine. But then it can turn so violent and ugly you would think the wrath of God was resting on it. When the wind blows hard out of the east the waves will get pushed up on the western shore and are just as pounding and vicious as the drumbeat of hell.

"Sometimes when the weather was clear and the day was pleasant, Sally would go out and stare toward the lake. We couldn't actually see it direct from the farm. She would just stare and wrap her shawl around her as if she were facing a blizzard. She would seem frozen and just keep staring. One day she finally told me what she saw. She saw the waves coming in a rush from the east. They were mounting up in a threatening heap and then she said that they just crashed over her and she couldn't move to get out of the way. Then she would get so tired and at night if I woke up I could hear her crying beside me in the bed."

Tom's lips began to quiver but he forced himself to continue with a choking voice. "I would hold her tight, Daniel, and rock her and try to tell her it was all going to be all right, but she would just cry herself to sleep in my arms. Sally knew that she hadn't seen any waves. She knew that she hadn't been crushed by them as they beat on the shore. But the experience was so real in her mind that she was just as tired and sore as if she had been trying to handle a little dinghy in a monster storm on the lake. You see, Daniel, you are like her. For you it is a buffalo stampede. You know there weren't any real buffalo out there. You've even gone to see that it is so. But it was real to you, as real in your mind as if there had been. Sally was so happy that she thought you understood her pain. I'm so happy I found her note. It was her last wish that I take care of you and I don't know what I would have done if I found that note too late. I will take care of you, son. I will take care of you." Then breaking down again he pulled Daniel to him and they stood silently together in the secure embrace of home.

The young man coming of age leaned back in his chair. He had found writing the reunion of Daniel and Tom to be exhausting. He felt an equal sense of relief, however, to have been able to pour his feelings into words. But were the words enough? Did Daniel now have all he needed? Had he escaped the damning words of the Reverend Stout or would everyone he ever met still cast the same stones of accusation against him? Was Reverend Stout's pronouncement going to still be his real fate? Was Tom the only friend he would need? Would a home with Tom really end his sadness or was Tom condemned to have the weight of Daniel and his fears and visions be just another mill stone around his neck?

The young man realized that these were not just Daniel's questions but also his own. Now Daniel had a home but the young man shuddered as he reflected that he was once again leaving his for school. He had tried to shut out the idea for the past few months. He had tried to combat his dread by quoting Scripture verses that spoke of God's constant presence. He had tried but he had failed to shake the ever increasing grip of apprehension that enveloped him. He knew that Daniel had to have answers, answers that would help the young man as well. Again he picked up his pen and turned to a new clean page.

Chapter 10
More than Home

The following week was a busy time for Tom and Daniel. Tom had found an outcropping of rock about a mile past where they were camped by Sally's grave. Time and weather had broken the outcropping into smaller rocks of varied sizes. Daniel received continued training in driving the team as they went to the pile each day and gathered quantities of stone for the gravesite. Using larger rocks they had formed a cross around the outside and then filled it to a handbreadth depth within the cross. They had also found a larger slap of stone about three feet long and just over a foot wide. Daniel had worked hard at crudely chiseling Sally's name on it and the year 1855. At the head of the cross they had dug a hole and set the slab upright in it with only a foot of the rock showing above the ground.

In the evenings they sat around the fire and Tom would read to Daniel from Sally's Bible. "I never paid much real attention to Sally's faith," Tom lamented. "A church social was a good place to meet a girl and that's how we met. It always meant a lot to her and I would go along each Sunday and rest and think about what had to be done on Monday. I don't think I ever did hear one whole message the reverend gave. The folks were nice and Sally always seemed so happy to go. Every night she read out of this Bible, Daniel, and I never once read it with her. Now, I'm going to read it to you. Or we can take turns, but I'm kind've afraid that if I left the reading to you my mind would wander just like on those Sunday mornings.

"But then as Sally got worse and the storms in her mind became fiercer she didn't go as often as before. For a while some ladies from the church would come and sit with her and try to cheer her, but she didn't cheer easily. After a while they stopped coming and I could hear the gossip in town as they talked about her. It soured me, Daniel. It soured me something awful to hear them talk about Sally. But Sally just went right on reading her Bible every night. On days when she didn't get up she would read it all day long. I watched her sometimes when she didn't know I was looking. She always seemed so peaceful, but she couldn't read all the time. But after each storm that she had she would still sit and read out of this Bible and seem at peace for a while at least. It will be like us being with her, I think, to read it each night like she did."

On the seventh night it rained, a great, powerful, thundering, prairie shaking rain. The morning of the eighth day dawned with a peace that rivaled the fury of the storm. Raindrops glistened in dazzling prisms on the prairie grass stems. Every bird awakened with joyful shouts of praise for the new clear day. As they had seen the storm approaching Tom and Daniel had rigged a trough along one side of their wagon and run it to the water barrels which were now overflowing. The horses snorted their appreciation for the dry dawn and drank deeply from the water that had formed a puddle under the barrels.

It was Tuesday and they had decided that this would be the day, if no other train came along, they would have to head out on their own to whatever place they might choose to stay. Neither Tom nor Daniel was eager to move away from the ground they found so sacred. They took their time clearing their campsite and preparing to set out. With unspoken consent they decided to eat lunch before pulling out. Having hearts heavy with leaving but tugged by the necessity of moving on they were climbing to the wagon seat when Daniel took one last glance back toward Sally's grave.

Above the marker he spied a distant small white cloud appearing over a small rise in the distance. He grabbed Tom's arm and pointed. The cloud had now become two and then three. Another wagon train was coming and the big schooner tops rose like clouds along the far horizon. Based on their own trail experience they knew that their new company would arrive at their site just about time to stop and camp for the night. They climbed down from their seat and unhitched the team. They each felt that indeed it was going to be a glorious day.

In late afternoon the other wagons came to a halt beside Tom's. There were only fifteen wagons in the group. Each wagon had two horses tethered to their back and several crates of chickens strapped to their sides. Behind the train came a small herd of dairy cattle, mostly young heifers with a few milking cows being herded by several men. Also attached to the rear of the lead wagon was a young bull. The newcomers watched with some apprehension as Tom and Daniel approached them. Were these two strangers just a ruse to waylay them for brigandage? Children who had been walking alongside the wagons now sought shelter on their far side from the strangers. Tom noticed the response and appreciated the uniqueness of their situation.

"Good afternoon, friends," he greeted them. "I'm Tom and this is Daniel. We're mighty happy to have you come along."

The driver of the lead wagon replied, "I am Johann Schmitt. Dit you break down?" Herr Schmitt spoke with a heavy German accent.

"My wife passed away a week ago. Wagon trains don't stop, but we decided to stay and care for our dead and wait for another train that we might join."

Herr Schmitt looked at the grave to which Daniel pointed. It was certainly not the work of just a few hours or quick burial. "Ver you going to Oregon? Ve are not going to Oregon."

Tom eyed their menagerie and replied, "I don't suppose with all these animals that you were planning to go so far. At one time we were but plans have changed. We are thinking about settling somewhere on this great prairie instead."

"Ah. Vell, zat is our intention, too. Ve plan to go up to ze Platte and move a little vest and set up a place vhere vagons can stop for rest and supplies."

As he spoke Daniel lost all attention to what was being said. From the wagon a head had appeared beside the man and then the slim form slipped down in the seat beside him. Daniel's eyes were riveted on the most beautiful creature he had ever seen. Her long brown hair and dark green eyes filled all his vision. Herr Schmitt did not fail to notice his daughter's disobedience in making herself known, nor did he miss a single aspect of Daniel's response.

"Katrina, you ver to stay in the vagon."

But the girl did not move. "Yes, Papa, but these men are not bandits. They are alone and very sad. Look at the grave, Papa. It was made with such care." As she spoke several of the men from other wagons had gathered to make an inspection of the two strangers. Two of them, speaking only in German, discussed the situation with Herr Schmitt. Daniel cared little for the conversation that he could not understand. He cared much, however, for the beautiful creature sitting next to Herr Schmitt. And much to his joy he noticed that she was also watching him as well and not listening to the others.

"Ve vill make camp here tonight," was the final pronouncement of Herr Schmitt. "Please join us in our meal," he extended the invitation to Tom and Daniel. Daniel pulled his eyes from Katrina and thanked him for his generosity.

As the women prepared the supper the children now again happily played around the wagons. Katrina had disappeared with the women. Two of the men from other wagons cut Tom away from Daniel as smoothly as an experienced cowboy could cut one dogey away from the herd. Daniel hardly noticed until the firm voice of Herr Schmitt called his name.

"Daniel, that is right, is it not?"

"Um, yessir."

"I vas young vonce. I know how a young man looks at a young girl. I haf seen how you looked at my daughter. I vant to stop vhat should not start. A young man must look first to the Papa. Ve are all Germans. Some of us have lived in America for many years. Some of us in our little group haf only come here recently. But ve are all Germans. Ve took daughters of German Papas for our vives. Ve vant to take sons of German Papa's for our daughters. Ve all have von fait. Ve are all Luterans. Do you have a German Papa? Are you a Luteran?"

Daniel was stunned by the abruptness of Herr Schmitt. "I, ah, uh, really don't know if I have a German Papa or not. We never really talked about it. Tom is not my Pa, I only wish he was. I don't know about Luteran," Tom mimicked the pronunciation of the unfamiliar word. "What is that?"

Now it was Herr Schmitt's turn to be stunned. "You haf never known a Luteran? Vell, you haf much to learn. Are you an orphan or haf you just run away from home to see the vest?"

Daniel decided that to be bold and honest was his only chance to get to know Katrina. "No, sir, I am not an orphan. No, sir, I did not run away. My pa sent me away because he said I belonged to the devil. Miss Sally, that's her over there in the grave, didn't seem to think that was true. I don't know. Miss Sally said she believed in God the Father Almighty maker of heaven and earth and in Jesus Christ. She was sick, sir, and that is as far as what she told me. Me and Tom read her Bible together every night. I don't know much beyond that. I went to Sunday school years ago, but the Reverend Stout said the devil had me and pa agreed. I only know that Miss Sally didn't think so and that I don't know. Since I don't really have anyplace I'm from except Wabash, I suppose I could be a German as well as the next guy. Since I don't know what a Luteran is, I suppose I should find out if I am one."

Herr Schmitt broke out into peals of laughter. He shook and clapped his hands. Several other men came running to see what the commotion was about. When Herr Schmitt regaled them with the tale they all joined his mirth.

"Vell said, Daniel," Herr Schmitt continued to chuckle. "Ve vill see if ve can make you a German and a Luteran, too." Then he again shook with laughter and the others all joined in with him. "Now, come and eat vit us. And if you talk vit Katrina, talk to her only in my presence." A stern look crossed his face but a wink and a soft glint came from his eye. Again with much laughter the group of men and Daniel went to where the meal had been prepared.

Chapter 11
Regrouping and Moving On

The young man coming of age slowly packed his things. He looked around the dorm room. No, it had never become even a home away from home, he thought. He saw nothing in it that he believed would ever provoke a fond memory for him. Once again he had failed to integrate into the society of school. His grades had fallen from the honors he had received to a bland level of mediocrity. His only regret was thinking what this departure would mean for his desire to serve in the ministry.

That, however, he concluded, was up to God. He laid no blame on God for not standing by Him. He knew that God had not left Him alone. He did not blame God for making him in such a way that something as easy as going away to school consistently proved impossible for him. He took one final look around and thought, God has made me; God has called me; God will lead me where I can go. With that he hauled his things to the waiting car and took the long trip home to face friends who might not be nearly as understanding as he had become of himself.

Darkness, the underlying day to day general sense of darkness had never left the young man. He had adopted Joshua 1:8-9 as his life passage. He had even written a song using those two verses. He never doubted their truth but he also never came out of the fog of darkness that enveloped him. Pushing against the pain he had finished the semester and dreaded what greater darkness might lie ahead of this repeated failure.

Winter's cold blasting wind beat against the window of his mother's apartment. Grey skies hung low over the dirty snow and occasional patches of brown grass. The young man coming of age alternately stared across the bleak scene and then tried to refocus on theology texts he was trying to read. Learning had not stopped when he left school, but the embrace of home had not relieved his darkness as it had in the past. Day after day he sat by the window and poured over the books he would have been studying at school. Day after day he cried from his darkness for light. Day after day the weak sun, if it even appeared, dropped below the horizon to bring on darker night.

The Bible study group he had so enjoyed no longer existed. His friends had, as young people so often do, moved for jobs or school or grown in to various church bodies in the city. They had become disconnected from each other. He had found it increasingly difficult to blend in with other new friends or make connections at his mother's church. Dark despair had slowly thrown its cloak completely over him and thoughts that had become almost forgotten again lapped at the corners of his mind.

It's a waste of time, the darkness would say, to keep on studying. It's a waste of time to hope for what you will never receive. It's a waste of time to believe in what you cannot see. It's a waste of time to think you serve a God who cares. Then he would hear the darkness laugh and say, maybe it's a waste of time just to be.

Steadily the young man read. Steadily the pile of books grew higher. Steadily he cried out for light. Spring came with more clouds and rain and wind. It brought with it neither warmth nor comfort. Steadily the voice said, it's a waste of time.

Spring approached summer and finally the sun shone. The young man ran into an old friend and they got an apartment together. It had but one window and that faced a garbage covered alley. Steadily the young man read. Kindly his mother had fed him and now kindly his friend was doing the same. Unkindly the voice daily said, it's a waste of time. The young man put down his book and went to the kitchen and pulled a knife from the drawer. Maybe the voice was right.

Bang! Bang! Bang! Someone was beating on his door. Without thought he carried the knife with him to answer it. A barely known neighbor stood there with a roll of pepperoni, a hunk of cheese and box of pizza mix. "Wow!" she blurted looking at the knife. "You must have known I was coming. Let's get this stuff sliced up and make some pizza." The moment passed; the visit passed; the young man steadily read on.

Summer's heat passed and the paper was filled with ads for school. The young man did the impossible. He made a decision. He would go to university. His grandmother lived in a town with a university. He would show up at her door and she would welcome him and he would be at home and he would go to school. All the thoughts raced together in his mind. She had raised him when he was little; he was sure she would want to do so again. And so he did.

Fall term began the day he arrived. He had his old room at his old home and he had gotten a job as janitor at his childhood church and a minister of music position at another church. Eight months of darkness evaporated as a dirty smog before a strong wind. He parked his car and stood at the edge of campus. Across the lot he was struck by the most beautiful creature he had ever seen. He had to meet her and he had to meet her now. Her long dark brown hair hung nearly to her waist. When he came face to face with her he was welcomed by her smiling green eyes. "Hi," she said. "Long time no see. Still studying for the ministry?" He merely nodded having no way to speak the words he wanted. Sensing an uncomfortable but not unpleasant silence she added, "We didn't really get very properly introduced the last time. My name is Beth." The young man remained speechless but smiled warmly at the introduction.

Days passed more swiftly than the needle on his grandmother's sewing machine. The young man's days were filled with a class load designed to finish a year and a half's work into one year. His nights were filled with working two jobs. But his life was filled with the young girl with sparkling green eyes. She agreed to sing in his choir, to encourage him in his studies for the ministry and to be his wife.

It was an absolute impossibility but he was absolutely sure that it was true; the days of darkness were past. Never again would they sweep across the blissful scenes of his life. Never again would they blot out the sun for days or months at a time. Never again would the voice mock him. There was only one thing he had to do to make sure it stayed just like it was. He had to make sure he never told her what kind of thoughts, what depths of darkness, what seeds of despair had really caused the setbacks he had faced earlier. It was gone. It was done. He knew; he was absolutely sure that God had filled the final hole in his life.

He had shared his darkness with no one. Once he had hinted at it to Dr. Connealy, but in the rush to go to school he had never made the second appointment. No one could ever come along and tell her anything more than that he had been a shy child. The past, the ugly dark past was gone. It was buried in her embrace. It was erased by the sparkle from her eyes. It was washed out to the depths of the sea by her own vivaciousness. Her gay, open love for people and life would cover for his uneasiness.

And then his grandmother died. The young man wandered through the silent empty house. Each room, each item in each room was full of the comfort of home, full of the safety of home, full of the assurance that he could step safely outside but also return. He came to the living room and sat in his favorite chair.

Then he stepped outside himself. He sat in the chair opposite from his own and tried to offer compassion and comfort to his hurting self. He tried to phrase truth that would ease the pain. He failed. He offered words of assurance that in the resurrection we meet our loved ones in Jesus again. He received a nod of assent. He counseled that we need not sorrow as those who have no hope. He was told he didn't understand.

"That is not my sorrow. It is in the other part of me; the part that only you know and now you want to escape it by sitting in that chair. This is the end of permanence. This house, her, everything here is the only permanence we have ever known. Have you forgotten so quickly our attempts at going off to college and leaving home? This time we didn't leave home. Home left us. The absolute stability of our entire being is dead. Dead! Don't sit over there and pretend it isn't so. Look around; all the security of sameness that has supported us for over twenty years is gone. It's not that we won't see her again; it's that we won't see her now. Every anxiety of separation that we have ever felt has now been filled to the brim. Every need we have ever had to do the same things and live the same way is gone. Every comfort we received from the sameness of her is dead. Don't sit over there and pontificate at me. Get over here and sit back in me and admit that we are doomed. Admit that we are without direction because the compass is broken."

"You're right; all that we have held on to for all these years is gone. We won't eat at that table any more. We won't open our Christmas presents in this living room any more. We won't walk up those front steps any more. But we are on the verge of beginning something that will last for us into the future. If our little Beth could see us sitting here and arguing she would be gone, too. We have the hope of love and making a new permanence. We have the joy of living it with someone we will love forever. Now, do you still want me to come over and sit with you in the past and panic or are you going to come over and sit with me in the future and hope? Come, let's grieve together. We will grieve much, but we will also live together with the hope of seeing Grandma again and having our own new beginning. Agreed?"

The young man joined himself in the other chair and together they wrapped their arms around his knees and buried their face on his chest. With deep, dry sobs he fell asleep while drifting into the safe corner of his imagination.

Chapter 12
Again and Again

By and large a wagon trip across the prairie could become a sameness that was mind numbing. Day after day the animals pulled creaking wagons across a landscape that varied little. The same food was eaten and same hot sun continued to beat down on the travelers. Water was in short supply; baths were few; animals became balky; patience became frayed; conversation became infrequent and often died on lips burnt by the sun. In every direction there was grass, grass and more tall waving grass. They were sixteen tiny boats afloat on a great green sea that undulated with the breeze or lay becalmed in the breathless air under a relentless sun. Every day there were two certainties – grass and sun.

But the evenings were different. Each night when all was settled, the meal finished and cleared, chores all done, Herr Schmitt would take his giant Bible and read to the assembled congregation. He would read from the Psalms and then a chapter from one of Paul's letters and then a story from the Gospels. He would read it all in German but Daniel and Tom listened as intently and respectfully as if they understood. After he had read from the Bible Herr Schmitt would take another large book, which Katrina told Daniel was Luther's Large Catechism and Augsburg Confession, and read a section from that. He read that more slowly and Katrina would translate it quickly for Daniel. After the readings they would all rise and make a group recitation of what Katrina told Daniel was the Apostles' Creed, the Ten Commandments and the Lord's Prayer. Then everyone in the circle around the fire reverently folded their hands and repeated Luther's Evening Prayer. Afterwards they went quietly to their wagons to rest for the next long day.

The day they reached the Platte they set camp early and rested. After a nap in the shade of his wagon Herr Schmitt searched out Daniel and asked him to walk with him along the bank of the river. "You and Herr Miller haf been goot companions for us. I am impressed, Daniel, at how much attention you haf giwen to ze readings ve haf each night. I know it must be hard since you don't understand, but you haf been respectful. So now I must know someting, perhaps someting you don't vant to tell me. I vatch you vit Katrina and you are alvays goot to her. You are alvays goot and obedient to Herr Miller. So, vhy, please tell my vhy, did your papa send you avay? Vhy did ze reverend tell you zat the devil had you in his hands?"

Daniel bowed his head. It was the moment he had feared, but since it hadn't come he had begun to hope that it wouldn't come. He shook his head and took out his handkerchief to wipe his nose and hopefully wipe his eyes as well without Herr Schmitt noticing.

"So, it brings you to tears, but you don't vant to tell me? Come now, Daniel. I haf not kept you from seeing Katrina every day. I haf not been unkind to you, haf I?"

Again Daniel shook his head, blew his nose and wiped his eyes. "No, sir. You have been kind. You have not kept me from sitting by Katrina at prayer time each night. I just don't know how I can tell you."

"All right, Daniel, vould you please answer my questions if I ask zem straightly? Did your papa know zat you had stolen someting and dishonored his name?" Daniel shook his head no. "Did your papa find you doing someting vicked vit a girl?"

"NO!" Daniel blurted out. "No! Never."

"Did you curse your mama or papa?" Daniel shook his head no. "Did you make some ugly little idol from vood and vorship it

behind the barn?" Daniel laughed, but when he saw that Herr
Schmitt was serious he shook his head no again. "Did you lie about
somevon and cause zem great harm?" Daniel silently responded no
again. "All right, Daniel, did you murder somevon?" Daniel looked
aghast at him and could not utter the exclamation of denial out
loud. Shaking his head violently he looked out across the river.
"Vell, zen Daniel, vhat did you do?"

"Herr Schmitt, I cannot tell you. I learned the Ten
Commandments in Sunday school and I have not broken them in
any big way. I have wanted things that weren't mine and I haven't
always told the truth and I'm awful sorry to have done those
things. I haven't always obeyed my ma and pa, and I know that
was wrong and I'm sorry for that, too. It's not for what I did, Herr
Schmitt. It's for who I am."

"Who you are? Vhat does zat mean? Are you a bastard child
of your father's sin or your mother's sin?"

Daniel turned in anger to his questioner. "No! They were
God fearing people."

"Zen vhat does it mean, 'who you are'?"

"I can't tell you. Maybe Tom can. He knows who I am. If
Miss Sally were still alive she could tell you clearly. I can't explain
to you who I am, but that is why I was sent away."

"Vell, zen Daniel, I haf jus von more question. If you
become a goot German and a goot Luteran, will who you are be
goot or bad for my Katrina?"

"I would love her always, Herr Schmitt. I would care for her
as my most prized possession. I would work hard to make sure she
was happy. Is that good enough?"

"It is nice vords, Daniel, and I beleef you mean zem. It is
not vhat I asked. I vill talk to Herr Miller. In ze meantime I vill not
make you change your vays vit Katrina." Silently they retraced
their steps back to the campsite.

Daniel was waylaid by Herr Schmitt's youngest son, Philip .
"Did you ask Papa for Katrina's hand, Daniel? Did he say yes?"

The simple question of the child caught Daniel by surprise.
His relationship with Katrina had certainly been noticed by all her
family. Maybe it was being talked about by everyone. He wouldn't

know because they all spoke German when he was around. "No, Philip ," he answered trying to sound happy and unconcerned. "We don't get much chance to talk on the trail, so we just had a nice talk now."

Philip laughed and skipped off singing to the other children on the train, "Daniel and Katrina, Daniel and Katrina." All the children laughed and joined in a circle singing the song.

As he approached their wagon Daniel could hear voices coming from the opposite side. One was the clear voice of Tom and the other the strong German accent of Herr Schmitt. Feeling guilty about eavesdropping, but compelled to hear what was said, Daniel tried to appear busy doing something quietly on his side of the wagon.

"I know you are concerned, Herr Schmitt. She is your daughter and we are strangers to you. Daniel is a good boy, or rather a good young man. It is just that he is little different than some people. He sees things with his heart more than his mind sometimes. He feels things that many of us don't feel at all. He's quiet and not one to mix well with others. He feels pain and sadness more than other people do. Sometimes that pain and sadness leave him weak and without a lot of energy. Sometimes he has more energy than five men.

"He's smart, too. He can read better than most people I have ever met. That's saying a lot since his pa took him out of school. His pa saw his sadness and his shyness and thought he was lazy. He thought that people who cried were not strong in body or mind. If they were weak in their mind then they had to be weak in their faith in God. If God could not cheer them up then they must belong to the devil. Is that what you wanted to know? I will tell you this, if I had a daughter, I would let Daniel court her in a minute."

"Tank you, Herr Miller. I understand vhy Daniel could not say zese tings." Coming around the wagon he spoke to Daniel. "Und now you haf heard, Daniel, vhat is spoken. I vill beleef Herr Miller. You can court my Katrina." Herr Schmitt returned to his wagon.

For five more days the little wagon train continued west along the Platte. Each day Daniel spent a few hours with a different man who spoke both German and English. As they rode in the wagon together he tried to learn to hear the German sounds from different voices. Repeatedly he dogged them with questions about words and slowly built a small vocabulary. Around the fire each night he asked if he could have a German Bible to follow along as Herr Schmitt read from his. When the evening recitations and prayers were made he tried to form the words on his own lips. He would show Herr Schmitt that he could be a "goot Luteran".

On the final night of their journey Herr Schmitt called Daniel aside when the service was over. "Daniel, you haf been doing wery vell. You haf started to learn to be a goot German. But, Daniel, being a goot Luteran is not just saying vords. No man is saved by goot vords. Vhen ve say zat ve beleef it is not to say ze vords but to speak our heart. Vhat ve beleef is tree tings. Von, ve beleef in von Gott who has made everyting. Ve beleef zat dis von Gott has sent His Son Jesus Christ to die for sinners, vhich ve all are. Vhen you did not obey your mama and papa, zat vas sin. Zat is vhy Christ died, to pay for your sin. Vhen ve tink evil of oters, zat is sin. Zat is vhy Christ died, to pay for zat sin. Ve all sin, Daniel, and ve beleef zat Christ has died to save us from all our sins. It is not vords, Daniel, it is beleefing. It is fait in Gott and in His Son Jesus Christ. Zen ve beleef zat ve are called to be living in a family called ze Church, put zere by God ze Holy Ghost. In your English Bible, Daniel, read in ze book of Romans chapters von to six. Zen read chapters tree tru fife again and again. Zen talk vit me in five days. Ve vill talk about how to be a goot Luteran. Goot night, Daniel, and may ze goot Gott bless you as you read."

Chapter 13
Joy and Understanding

The following afternoon the small train of wagons reached their destination. Herr Schmitt and his group had made a heavy investment and purchased four square miles of land at a dollar and a half per acre. It had been a tremendous strain on their combined resources, but now it was their land and their future. They brought their wagons to a halt and knelt down and gave thanks to Almighty God for their safe journey and new home. Rising from their knees they sang *Ein Feste Burg* and recited the Apostles' Creed.

Daniel and Tom had been invited to stand with Herr Schmitt's family during the ceremony which was entirely conducted in German. The solemnity of the service had kept Katrina from offering any translation to Daniel. After the Apostles' Creed was finished everyone was told to sit down and the first town hall meeting was held without a town hall. Again it was conducted only in German but this time Katrina translated.

"We have arrived, dear friends, by the grace of God and through His care. I will lay out what must come in the next few days. First we must eat!" Soft laughter came from the gathered families. "Then we must choose just the right spot to build our station. We will look over our land carefully and then choose wisely. Then we must get our families settled with suitable shelter for the next few months. Afterwards those who are to return to

Missouri for the extra supplies we will need can go. Tonight we will eat and rest; the children can run freely on their new land. Tomorrow we will begin in earnest to get these things done so that those returning to Missouri can do so and be back in time to help us all prepare for winter. I think that is all."

A surge of unexplained excitement ran through Daniel. He wasn't part of them, but he was overwhelmed with a feeling that he was, at that moment, a real part. Propelled by that sensation he raised his hand. "Yes, Daniel," Herr Schmitt continued in German, "What do you want to say?"

"Shouldn't we do one more thing, Herr Schmitt? Shouldn't we think of a name for our new home?" There, he had said something that wasn't really true. He had said "our new home", but was it? His mind reeled at his sudden audacity to even speak but then also claim a true part in the community. While his mind raced Herr Schmitt translated his words to the gathered families.

"Well, Daniel, perhaps you have an idea."

He didn't correct me, Daniel thought. He didn't scold me for my presumption. He looked around at all the faces now intently looking at him. In none of them did he find resentment or anger at his impertinence. "Herr Schmitt," he began uncertainly. "All these families are German and Luteran." Only the few children who had had non-German playmates and had lost some of their accent could hear his continued mispronunciation. They giggled and were quickly hushed by their parents.

Daniel was a little confused by the children's response but plunged on. "It should be a name that belongs to everyone. Everyone who has spoken to me always speaks of Dr. Luter." Again a chorus of giggles ran through the children. Again he paused in confusion and increasing embarrassment. But since everyone still looked at him he manfully went on. "Katrina," and at the mention of her name his face turned a deep crimson. Even the adults now joined in light laughter. Daniel felt the instant urge to flee but before he could make his feet follow his mind Herr Schmitt raised his hand for silence.

With growing terror and desperation Daniel looked at Herr Schmitt and then his family. Katrina smiled at him and nodded encouragement. "Katrina," he repeated, "has told me that Dr. Luter's first name was Martin." Heads nodded as the translation was made for all. "Maybe, we," there was that familiar word again. Daniel shuddered. What am I saying? There is no "we". In five days there may be no me. What if I can't tell Herr Schmitt what he wants to hear? What am I doing even trying to speak? I can't speak to these people. I can't do what I'm doing. What am I doing? I am making a fool of myself. A haze slowly formed before his eyes. His chest pounded and he struggled to breathe. He opened his mouth but no more speech came.

Then gently on his arm he felt the hand of Katrina. He turned to her trying to control his fear and anxiety. He could hear the others beginning to murmur, murmur in German. Were they making fun of him? Another strong hand rested on his now shaking shoulder. He turned and through the haze he saw Tom. It looked like Tom was drowning, gasping for breath, but as he focused he saw that Tom was simply talking to him. "It's all right, Daniel. Everyone is concerned if you are all right. You are all right. You are doing a fine job of talking. Just finish your idea. Everyone looks like they want to hear it."

But Daniel did not finish. He buried his face in Tom's shoulder and began to sob, great wracking sobs while his body shook uncontrollably. I am finished, his thoughts raced through his anguished brain. I am finished here. Katrina cannot want a weeping boy like me. The others will look at me with scorn and hide their children from me. They will say, see that boy, the devil has him by his nose and by his toes; don't go near him lest the devil get you too. They will not let Tom and me stay here any longer. We will have to live up the river until the next train comes by. Oh, if I just had my knife I could end all the pain.

But through the sound of his own sobs he could hear from a great distance, farther it seemed to him than the blue line of the far horizon, he could hear the clear music from a crystal music box. It was singing words that he could not understand but which sang like peace in his soul. The crystalline chimes drew ever closer until they hung above his head. He pulled his face from Tom's shoulder and looking up through the prism of tears saw Katrina standing beside him.

"We all know that Daniel doesn't speak German very well yet. He is unfamiliar to us and us to him. He says the name of our faith as he hears us say it." Then smiling at the younger children who had laughed at him, "but these children can hear what many others here cannot hear. He pronounces the name of our faith incorrectly, and finding it cute I never corrected him. So the children who hear in English but speak in German know it sounds funny coming from Daniel." Then looking down at Daniel she continued. "It is Lutheran, Daniel, not Luteran."

Daniel gasped at his stupidity. How foolish he must have seemed to all these people. What a fool he had always been and always would be. He was the laughingstock of children and the fearful one among the adults. Oh, if he could just hide, break away from Tom's embrace and flee to the wagon and get his knife and hide forever. But Tom held him firmly and Daniel saw in his eyes the look he had often seen Tom give to Sally. He sagged against Tom's chest.

Katrina was continuing. "Daniel told me last night that he thinks we should call our settlement Martinsville after Dr. Luther because he is someone we all respect and admire." Then turning toward her father she said, "I am sorry Papa for standing to speak without your permission. I just wanted to finish what Daniel was saying." She again sat down.

Herr Schmitt's eyes swelled with tears of pride and tenderness. He wiped his nose and spoke to the families in German. "Daniel has presented a good idea, I think. What say all of you?" Heads nodded and a voice of assent rose from the assembly.

Daniel stared in amazement at the people around him. There was no flinching away from him. There were no mothers hiding their children. He was greeted with smiles and words of thanks for offering up such an idea that would honor them all. His head told him that he was small and foolish for his actions and inability to say something so simple. His heart, however, received warmth from the approval of his new friends.

"You did well, Daniel," Tom said as he patted him on the back. "You did real well."

Katrina turned to him and smiled. "It is a good name, Daniel. Thank you for choosing it."

Herr Schmitt's voice silenced the others. "Then we will have our first evening meal in Martinsville. It will be a grand place to the glory of Gott the Father Almighty."

Chapter 14
Meeting of Minds and Hearts

Days of the succeeding week were filled with constant activity and the nights were filled with exhaustion. Daniel slumped to his bedroll sleeping before he was laid down. Then shaking the utter weariness from his mind he would crawl out again and sit by the fire with Miss Sally's Bible and read what Herr Schmitt had told him to read. Crawling again into his blanket he would sleep before he could think through what he read.

Each dawn was welcomed with the clattering of pans as the women fixed breakfast. Sore from more labor than he had ever done Daniel would grope his way to the cool waters of the Platte and bury his face in them until he could hold his breath no longer. Awake, but not refreshed, he would return to his wagon and again try to read his assigned lesson before the meal. Fed but not refreshed Daniel would return to the small grove of cottonwood trees slightly upstream. There the trees, some giants of ancient age were being thinned out. The oldest and biggest would come down and give way for new growth to provide the needs for the settlement's future.

Tom explained to him that this was certainly not the best wood to build with, but on the prairie you had to use what you had until there was better. It was soft and not durable but it should get them through the winter. At that comment Daniel shuddered in his heart. All this work would have to be done again. There was chopping and splitting and hauling. Even the children were busy picking up the remains to be used for future firewood. It was bad firewood Tom had explained, but it did burn warmer than snow. Other men had been busy breaking up the thick and heavy sod to make a place to put new buildings. As Daniel watched them try to cut through the nearly six foot deep roots of the tall prairie grass he was glad that his job was cutting wood.

Each night they gathered inside the circle of wagons that had become their temporary home and had their evening service. Daniel's work roughened hands would stiffly open the Bible and he tried to follow along with Herr Schmitt without falling asleep. Sometimes he would try unsuccessfully and be nudged by either Tom or Katrina who were themselves at the borderland of exhaustion. With the conclusion of Luther's Evening Prayer no one lingered and the deep tones of sleep soon wafted across the wide prairie.

Sunlight, real sunlight, not dawnlight but real sunlight splashed across Daniel's face. He opened his eyes but knew that he was dreaming. The camp was quiet. Too quiet. He sat up with a jerk. Had they all left him? Was he still lying alone on Miss Sally's grave? Had all those hopes and joys and days of painful labor been a joke his tormented mind had played on him?

He rubbed his eyes to clear the fog in them and looked around. The wagons were still there. Here and there he could see mothers sitting by the sleeping forms of their small children and caressing them gently. Intermingled with the sweet song of morning birds he could hear the distinct hum of male voices. He rolled under the wagon and sat up looking at the river. There were men standing in the water stripped to the waist and washing with soap. Soap, Daniel was amazed. He hadn't seen soap for a month, at least not on a human body. He stretched and strode down to the river and enjoyed a real bath if only a half bath.

Then it occurred to him to ask why no one was working. "It is ze Sabbat. Today ve rest. On ze trail ve had to keep going, but not today. Today, in our new home, ve celebrate our first Sabbat. Today ve rest."

Another man chimed in the conversation. "Yes, Daniel, today you can take your Katrina and valk out on ze prairie. But don't go too far from the eyes of Herr Schmitt." The other men laughed and Daniel supplied them with more fodder by his bright blushing face.

Clean, refreshed and rested the men returned to the camp and they all moved to the far outside of the wagons most distant from the river. The women and children then moved down and had their own baths and returned to lay out a cold breakfast. Herr Schmitt stood and called for them to come to worship. It was a service like none that Daniel had ever seen. They stood, they knelt, they sat, they sang and stood and sat some more. Herr Schmitt didn't just read from the Bible and a book, but he spoke to them and even waved his hand in the air.

As Daniel saw the hand raised he shuddered and was dragged in his mind back to the log cabin church in Wabash. The Reverend Stout was moving into the glory land part of his sermon. Not many were going there so everyone should show more true contrition for their sins and live their lives to prove that they were the ones who were. Then he would enumerate the many sins that would keep people from that place of rest. He would always get to sloth or to the blight of unhappiness and look at Daniel. Then he would warn them all that the devil was ready to take them by their nose and by their toes to eternal damnation if they let such sins cling to them.

Daniel shuddered again and Katrina looked with concern at the pall of fear that was spreading over his features. After more prayers and a song they were dismissed and Katrina pulled Daniel aside. "What was the matter with you? You looked like you were staring at a stampede of buffalo and couldn't get out of the way."

Daniel gasped and pushed Katrina's hand from his arm. "Don't ever say that," he snapped. "Don't ever say that to me again." Then seeing the shock on her face and feeling the dagger of doom digging in his heart he turned to run away. But as he turned he ran directly into Herr Schmitt.

"Daniel, vat is your tiff vit Katrina? Is that how you talk to her?"

Daniel spun to look at Katrina and saw the tears of hurt in her eyes. Turning back to Herr Schmitt he saw a look that brought him a greater darkness of woe. Turning quickly back to Katrina he stammered, "I'm so sorry, Katrina. It is something that happened long ago and," he paused and shook his head. "And I can't explain it. I'm sorry for speaking to you like that. I offer no excuses. I was wrong. Please forgive me."

"I do, Daniel. Now I think Papa wants to talk to you." She drifted off to help the women and the men walked off across the prairie.

"Your five days are up, Daniel. Have you read vhat I told you every day?"

"Yes, Herr Schmitt. Even when I forgot and went to bed without doing so I would get up and sit by the fire and read. Then I would read again each morning."

"Yes, I know. I vatch you, Daniel. I vatch you for ze sake of my Katrina. Now tink, Daniel, tink about vhat you haf read. You haf read dat Gott says all men are sinners. Do you tink you are a sinner, Daniel."

"I just was, sir. I was just rude to Katrina. I hurt her and that was sin. Right?"

"Yes, Daniel. Ve say unkind tings and hurt oters. Yes, zat is sin. Ve are all guilty before Gott and condemned by our sin. Did you see zat in vhat you read?" Daniel nodded. "Vell, vould you take the punishment for someone else who did to Katrina vhat you did? Vould you say to him, I saw you be unkind to my Katrina and hurt her but I vill take ze punishment from Herr Schmitt for you?"

"No! I would want to hit him and make him pay for that. He shouldn't have, I mean I shouldn't have done that."

"Goot, Daniel, wery goot. Sin should be punished. But Gott, He loved us, oh, He loved us so much zat He gave His Son Jesus to pay the punishment for our sin. Jesus was nefer unkind. He nefer sinned. But Gott took all our sins, Daniel, and He put zem on ze back of His own Son and made His own Son to die for your sins and mine. Vould you take ze first son of you and Katrina and take him to ze biggest jail vit ze vorst criminals, murderers and robbers and say, Here, take my son and kill him but let zem go free?"

Daniel blanched at the very thought. "Impossible! Never! No one would do that!"

"But, Daniel, ze goot Gott did zat for you and me and Katrina and everyone. Did you read zat?"

"I did, but I didn't understand it like that. God did that for me?" Herr Schmitt nodded. "Why? Why would he do it for me? I can see why He might have done it for you, Herr Schmitt, but not for me. The devil had my hand, Herr Schmitt. You heard Tom tell you. Why would God do that for me?"

"Daniel, I am no better zan you. Ve are all sinners. The devil has us all by ze noze and by ze toez. But God sent His Son to break ze chains zat hold us to ze devil. He sent His Son to save us and gif to us forgiveness and eternal life. If Katrina had said zomting zat hurt you and zen she came and said, Daniel, I am so sorry, please forgive me and keep me as your future vife, vould you forgive her, Daniel?"

"I would in an instant. I love her, Herr Schmitt."

"And the goot Gott loves you, Daniel, and if you come to Him and ask Him to forgive you because you beleef zat His Son has died for you, He vill forgive you too."

Daniel stared at Herr Schmitt in momentary disbelief but then it all became clear to him. The good God had indeed sent His Son to die for his sins and He did love him and would forgive him. Tears of relief and joy poured from his eyes. "I see," he choked. "I see it so clearly. I do believe, Herr Schmitt. I do believe that God has done that for me. Thank you. Oh, thank you for telling me. That means that I am forgiven for my sins. That means that the devil doesn't have me by the nose and by the toes anymore." He started to laugh while he cried. "The devil doesn't have me anymore." Then in a gesture so quick and unexpected that he could not stop himself Daniel grabbed Herr Schmitt and hugged him tightly.

"Daniel," Herr Schmitt spoke softly while he pulled himself from Daniel's embrace. "After our meal you can take Katrina on a short valk and zen you must bott come and talk vit me. Ze meal is ready. Let us return so zat all can eat."

Chapter 15
Confrontation

Old Sol hung like a golden globe draped in a mantle of pristine blue that cascaded to the horizon in every direction. A soft breeze gently swayed the tall grass and gave relief from the heat of the day. Daniel and Katrina walked hand in hand along the bank of the Platte upstream and away from the others. When they reached the small bend in the river that would obscure them from Herr Schmitt's view they turned from the riverbank and strolled up into the grass and completed the return circuit back to the assembled wagons.

Daniel told Katrina of the talk he had had that morning with her father. He told her of the joy he had in understanding what their faith meant to him. Before reaching a spot where they could be clearly heard from the encampment Daniel turned to Katrina and spoke softly but earnestly. "Katrina, Ich liebe dich. If your father says "yes", will you marry me?"

She turned to him and her green eyes were misty. "O, Daniel, Ich liebe dich. Yes. If Papa says we can, yes."

Suddenly more self conscious at the nearness of the others Daniel dropped her hand from his. Philip came skipping out from the wagons at the head of a group of children. "Daniel and Katrina, Daniel and Katrina," they sang. Pulling some of the heads off the tall grass the children showered the couple and then ran giggling and singing back into the safety of their parents. Other couples, some keeping their youngest children in tow, were also moving out for a walk on the prairie or down by the river.

Such a beautiful day and such peace, Daniel thought. Will it carry over to our talk with Herr Schmitt? Herr Schmitt had improvised a chair for himself within the small piece of shade afforded by his wagon and watched them approach. "Come, Katrina and Daniel, ve must find a place to speak more priwately." Then he led them in the direction of down river.

The other families and children sensing the importance of the impending conversation with Daniel and Katrina moved off in directions opposite of that which they had taken. Several hundred yards downstream they came to a small shelf of ground that was level and sat about six feet above the river. Herr Schmitt sat down on the short grass that grew on the shelf and the young couple followed his example. "I haf a few qvuestions," he began and looked at his daughter.

"Katrina, you are a beautiful young voman. You are older zan my moter ven she was betroted to my father. You are just von year younger zan your mama ven ve vere married. I see zat you haf begun to tink of such tings for your own life. Zat is ze vay of life. But, are you ready to tink such tings? Are you ready to take zis man vit all ze troubles as vell as all ze hopes zat may come? I vill gif you some qvuestions to tink about. Answer zem honestly.

"Katrina, vould you still loff Daniel if he lost a leg?"

Katrina was surprised at the question. She had imagined many questions that her papa could have asked, and that wasn't on the list. She looked at Daniel and replied, "Yes, Papa."

"Katrina, vould you still loff Daniel if he lost an arm?"

She stared at her father with perplexity. What kind of questions were these. Herr Schmitt raised his eyebrows and slightly tilting his head awaited her answer. "Yes, Papa."

"Katrina, vould you still loff Daniel if he lost an eye?"

The young girl grew increasingly confused by the nature of the questions. She stretched her arms out at an angle signifying her confusion. "Papa, why do you ask such questions?" He sat and looked at her without answering. Sighing with frustration she softly spoke, "Yes, Papa, I would." Then in exasperation she rushed on, "If he lost both eyes and both legs I would still love him."

Herr Schmitt bestowed a warm smile upon her. "You are a goot girl, my little Katrina. A wery goot girl und I beleef you. But I have von more qvuestion. You are my only daughter. You are ze joy of your moter and me. You haf seen in our home how a man leads his family. Vhat if Daniel lost his ability to lead your family? Vhat if he became unable to make a decision zat needed to be made? Vhat if he could not get out of bed von morning and just laid zer und cried? Zen, my darling Katrina, vould you still loff him?"

Katrina turned to stare at Daniel who had seemed to turn to stone beside her. His face was flushed and his breathing seemed to have stopped altogether. He was looking past her father to a point too distant for her to comprehend. Daniel's fingers had dug deeply into the grass and his knuckles were pale white under his well tanned skin. She tried to read the face of the man to whom she had just professed her love. It was neither angry nor sad. It was set as firm chiseled stone. Slowly his eyes moved from their distant focus and looked into her soul. They looked, and she knew that look, they looked lost. They looked like the eyes of the two small children back in Pennsylvania who stood by the grave of their parents who had died when their cabin burned. What lay ahead for them? What would they do? They stood there without tears but in the grip of the terror of being lost, completely lost, in a vast and dark forest without hope.

Katrina reached out her hand and placed it on his. Tears streamed down her smooth cheeks as she began to sense the pain and terror that now gripped her Daniel. Yes, he was HER Daniel, she thought, but where had he gone? Her heart raced. Where indeed had he gone? Could he come back to her from wherever it was? She tightened her grip on his hand. She quickly thought of the several boys who had wanted to court her back in Pennsylvania but whom she had asked her papa to send away. But not Daniel. Where he had gone she was sure she would go, to wherever it was to bring him back to her. "Yes, Papa. Yes, I would," she cried. "I would!"

She could feel Daniel's hand relax under hers. Somewhere in the back of his eyes she could see him returning. She placed her other hand on top of the one already holding his. The muscles in his jaw slowly slackened. His flushed face returned to the deep brown tone baked there by the bright Nebraska sun. Slowly his eyes swiveled to Herr Schmitt.

"Yes, Daniel," Herr Schmitt acknowledged his gaze, "you must tell her ze troot. If you had only von hand she could see it. If you had only von leg she could see it. She vould see ze troot and know vhat she vas getting. Now, you must tell her ze troot. It is not Herr Miller's job to tell her. It is yours and now is ze time."

Daniel shifted his position and sat cross-legged in front of Katrina. He took both of her hands in his. Bowing his head for a moment to gain composure to speak then he raised it and looked fully into her beautiful green eyes.

"Katrina, ich liebe dich. Papa is wise, very wise. These past few weeks have been the most wonderful in my life. In the sunshine of your presence I have felt the darkness that has held me for so long start to melt away. But somewhere in the back of my heart and mind I know it is still there. It is silent but it lurks like a thief with a heavy weapon to strike me down. I can't see him now or feel him now, but he is there just the same. Your joy has made me forget him for a while. I would like to forget him forever, but I don't know if that is possible. It wasn't possible for Miss Sally. Maybe it isn't possible for anyone.

"I was sent away from home because the Reverend Stout said that the devil had me by the nose and by the toes. My pa believed him. He knew that on some days I just couldn't get up and going like he wanted. Some days I would be in the field and just start crying. I couldn't talk to other people or stand in class and recite my lessons. Aside from the lessons it wasn't like that every day or even most days. But when it was I, well, I just couldn't get a hold of myself and so the Reverend said that was because someone else already had a hold of me. Pa said he wouldn't feed a person forever who was on their way to perdition, so he sent me away.

"The night after Miss Sally died I was staying by her grave. Then I heard a rumble and the earth shook. The moon was bright as day and I looked all around to see what was happening. In the distance there was a herd of buffalo, there must have been a million of them, and they were charging across the prairie right at me. I laid down on Miss Sally's grave and felt their sharp hooves trampling over me. I felt their weight crushing me into the ground. I couldn't breathe. But the next morning the sun was shining and I was alive. But if it weren't for Tom I'd be dead. What the buffalo didn't finish killing I was going to finish. It wasn't the first time I had ever felt that way, but it was the worst time and I just didn't think I could go on. That is why I got so suddenly angry when you said I looked like I was being charged by a herd of buffalo.

"Now I can still see an old bull buffalo just standing at the edge of my life and slowly chewing his cud. But he has his eye on me. Behind him is his whole herd. Right now he is just eating, but he is there. Someday when the fire comes into his eyes and he leads his herd down upon me again, will you still want me?"

Katrina tried to choke back her quiet sobs in order to speak. "Daniel," she choked, "I will be there to wash your bloody wounds and pour salve into every cut they leave on you. I will nurse you back to health and if they come again I will do it again and again and again. Ich liebe dich, Daniel. Ich liebe dich."

Herr Schmitt intruded into their reverie. "Daniel, do you vant to haf my Katrina for your vife?" Daniel had become too overwhelmed with emotion to speak but nodded yes.

"Katrina, vould you still haf Daniel as your husband." Through streaming tears she nodded yes. "Then ve vill haf a vedding on your sewenteenth birthday next April."

Chapter 16
Herr Schmitt's Story

"Now, children," Herr Schmitt continued, "I need to tell you a story. A true story. Daniel, I vill tell it in German because vhen I tink of it, I tink of it in German. I vill go slowly and Katrina can translate if for me."

It began in the time of the French Revolution and Napoleon. Europe was in turmoil. My father was a squire for a young prince from Hess, a German region. My father's family was from East Friesland, and he had joined the army when he was fifteen to help support the family. He had moved from stable hand up to the prince's squire. He had been near many battles and the prince had told him that the good preparation of his horse had saved his life more than once.

When my father was thirty, even though the wars with Napoleon were still raging, the prince gave him a month's leave to go home. While there he was betrothed to my mother who was fourteen at the time. He still had five years service to complete and then they would be married. He and the prince both survived the next five years and his service was done. The prince was so pleased with how he had served that he gave my father what amounted to a small treasure.

My father was a devout Lutheran. He had always had some Lutheran pamphlets that he read and reread. The prince had noted that. When my father was discharged the prince gave him a library of Dr. Luther's books. He gave him a library of ten books by Dr. Luther and other early Lutheran teachers. In those days such a library was worth a fortune. He also gave my father enough gold to buy a good farm.

When my father returned home he discovered that many Calvinists had moved into his area. Some Lutheran families had even intermarried with them. My father gathered together thirty families who were committed to Lutheranism, which isn't called that in Germany; in Germany it is called the Evangelical Church. He agreed to lead them to America to join a German Lutheran settlement here. They secured passage on a ship and arrived in America in the summer of 1811. I was born that autumn.

They had immediately set out for Pennsylvania where other Germans lived. They worked for them through the winter and then bought and settled their own farms in the spring. Each year a few more settlers came to our area most Lutheran but some not. Then just before1850 there had been great turmoil in Europe again. Revolution was in the air and there was a new wave of immigrants. Some of the families with us are part of those new immigrants. But now there were also many more people who were not German or Lutheran and I felt we should do as my father did and restart a strong Lutheran community. Today Daniel you have given your confession and next Sunday I will baptize you. Then I will train you to be a good Lutheran.

But now we must return to my boyhood in Pennsylvania. I had a wonderful friend, a true and dear friend named Philip. He had been born while our families were still at sea on the way to America. Our farms abutted each other. While Philip was my best friend, I was probably his only friend. It is after him that I have named my own son. He was very shy. About age thirteen he began to change from just being shy to being really separate from others. Pastor Straussen talked with him and prayed with him and gave him some ideas how he might feel better. Philip followed Pastor's advice and showed some improvement. But it was only some improvement.

Then one day I was going to see him and his mother told me he had gone into the forest. I knew where he might be because we had played at Indians there many times. Still playing like an Indian I snuck up on where I saw him sitting. His head was bowed and I then thought he might be praying so I even more quietly approached. But he wasn't praying; he was crying, not a little but in giant sobs that wracked his body. Except when we were small children and got hurt I had never seen Philip cry. I sat down beside him and when he looked at me I wanted to cry, too.

I asked what the matter was and he told me he had seen a hawk catch a rabbit. The rabbit had screamed and Philip said the scream got louder and louder until it filled the whole forest with its terror. He asked if I couldn't hear the scream myself. Well, I could not. But I told him I had heard such a scream when a rabbit or squirrel was caught by a hawk. I agreed it was a sad sound. He just nodded his head and continued to cry. I did something I had never done before. I hugged him to me until he stopped.

Then he told me he could hear that sound sometimes at night when he couldn't sleep. An owl had snatched another meal, but the screams of its prey lasted longer than they should and were so loud he thought everyone in the cabin should be awake. One night he had opened the shutter at the end of his loft and looked out. The moon was full and he was sure he saw a man, but not just any man. The man looked like half man and half monster. He looked up at Philip just as he had opened the shutter and glared at him. His eyes were red and his mouth was wide and vicious looking. Philip had slammed the shutter tight and spent a sleepless night. Every night afterwards he slept with a knife.

Over the next few months Philip was often sick and missed school. He didn't have a fever or anything the doctor could find, but his body ached and he was listless. One day soon after that he came to school and was the happiest I had ever seen him. He even talked to the other students and even talked to Hannah Straussen, the Pastor's daughter. He was like that for a whole week, almost two. The next day he was sick again and when I went to see him after my chores his mother told me he had felt well enough to go into the forest. I knew where and went to find him. I did find him and I shall never forget it. (Here Herr Schmitt paused, shuddered and began to cry himself. After regaining his composure and drying his eyes, he continued.) But I didn't find him in time.

Katrina gasped and clung more tightly to Daniel's hands. "Yes, Katrina", Herr Schmitt continued in German, "he was dead."

He was covered in his own blood. He had cut his wrists and bled to death all alone in the forest. I fell on him and wept and wept and wept. It was almost dark when I got up and then I too was covered with his blood. I staggered to his cabin and when his mother saw me she knew right away what had happened. His papa made me lead him to the body and then brought him home before animals could do him damage. His older brother Conrad had been sent to get Pastor Straussen while we went into the forest. Pastor Straussen's wife and my mother were called to help his mother and to prepare Philip for burial.

By that time our community had some non-Lutheran settlers. Maybe, really, they made up almost half of our population. Sometimes I forget how soon things had changed. We Lutherans had kept pretty much to ourselves so; while the others were there they had not really impacted our lives. Our school was run by the vicar and non-Lutheran families had started their own school. Anyway the news of Philip's death and how it happened soon spread to the whole town. I heard such things as I never wanted to hear again, but Daniel has reminded me of them all. Yes, Daniel, what Reverend Stout told you I heard many times in many unkind ways. We Lutherans were surely not a people of faith to let such goings on happen in their midst. On and on it went for many months.

Pastor Straussen gave us a different comfort than the horrors we heard from our neighbors. Philip was buried in our church cemetery with a proper Christian funeral. Pastor Straussen told of a story about Dr. Luther. One time a boy had committed suicide. Yes, children, it is an old problem. The sexton would not let the boy be buried in the cemetery. Certainly, he said, it would leave all the others in the cemetery damned as well. Dr. Luther had responded that if the boy had been waylaid by highwaymen and killed he could have a proper Christian burial to which the sexton agreed. Then Dr. Luther said that we could not ban a proper

Christian burial to one who had been waylaid by the devil and killed by him. Then he told the sexton to give him the shovel and he would bury him himself.

For a month Pastor Straussen comforted our congregation with stories of Dr. Luther's care for those he said were depressed. Suicide, Dr. Luther said, was certainly never God's will for us, but that we all made choices that God would rather we did not. Those choices did not mean we had no faith. They meant that at that moment we listened to our flesh instead of God's spirit. What happened did not mean that Philip, who had given clear testimony of his faith throughout his life, had not been admitted into the arms of His Savior. We should all draw comfort from the good grace of God in the great trials of life.

To this day I miss my dear friend Philip. But, and it may seem strange to you having heard this story, I will not ban your marriage. Now my Katrina knows how you feel. No one knew how Philip felt but me, and I promised him I would tell no one. Katrina can pray for you when you can't even pray for yourself, Daniel. She can comfort you because she knows who you are. In a strange way, Daniel, I think I can make up what I owe to Philip by giving you a chance to a life with a good wife. May the good God give you each an abundance of happiness and may I, by the grace of God, live to see it take place for Philip's sake.

"Now, children, let us return to the others." They rose together, and Daniel and Katrina, hand in hand again, walked back to the encampment with Herr Schmitt.

Chapter 17
Awake and in Doubt

The young man coming of age swam to the surface of consciousness. No longer was he sitting in the chair where he had met himself in sorrow. There he sat, at his desk, unaware of the time or means by which he had moved. Beneath his hand he found the stack of pages scrawled in his own hand. Breathlessly he read through them and then once again. Good for Daniel, he thought. It is my little green eyed darling that is bringing me out of the darkness as well. Then he sighed as he reread the final few paragraphs of the story he had just written. If only I could tell her as Daniel was forced to tell Katrina. But this is just a story. It is the creation of my desires and my escape. I can make Daniel be forced to tell and I can make her respond with kindness and affirmation of their love.

Stories are so nice, but I live in a reality. Well, maybe I live in reality sometimes. I doubt very much that Beth would be so amicable. Who would? I'm a freak. Everybody looks up to me and respects me as some kind of giant spiritual leader. How many would turn and run if they knew that such thoughts still tug at my brain? How many would still listen if they knew I spent more time in my imagination than in reality? It is no different here than it was that night at the Bible study. No one really bought into my answer concerning suicide. They couldn't argue, but it was clear they wanted to. I still hear it all around. Depression is just a lack of faith. Suicide is, as Wesley said, an execrable sin that can be cured by shaming the dead. No, Beth loves who she thinks she knows, who I have been since I met her. But she has no idea who I remain in the corners of my mind. I just have to hope it doesn't show up again, that with her I really am better.

But, you fool, you aren't. The young man spun around and confronted himself sitting on the bed beside the desk.

I thought we had agreed to stay together, the young man responded.

Only if you aren't going to play the fool! Better! Hah! Don't ever count on better. Count on not telling her so that she won't freak out, but not on better. We're nothing without her. You can pass it off as a bad case of the flu, a little bit of weather related ennui or make up a story. You are good at stories. We'll be OK if we keep our mouth shut. But we won't be better.

The young man sighed and agreed. The two again embraced into one. He looked at the clock on his desk. It was four a.m. Some family members would be arriving from out of town by shortly after breakfast. He gathered his papers together and stuffed them quickly into the portfolio on top of an already packed box. Two days were left before the funeral. In three days his aunts and mother had said the house must be clean and empty. For him it was already empty. What it was was gone. But maybe, he thought, I can hang on to it if my little Katrina would agree to getting married right away instead of after graduation this spring. Maybe Grandma's essence, or maybe just her aroma, will hang in the air and I can breathe in her love. And, he had a bright and happy thought; if we get married right away there is no way Beth will see my collapse into protoplasm and beg off before May.

Energized he finished packing his room and started packing a few items that he knew his brother and sister would also want. Everything else was up for grabs, unless, and the happy thought came again, we can get married right away. Then we will just keep all these things and I can live happily ever after.

Fat chance, came the voice in his ear.

Shut up, was his quick reply. I can dream, can't I?

Oh, yeah, you can dream and that's all it amounts to. Just remember that.

After packing the few things he had selected he took a quick shower and waited for the family to come. It wasn't really them he awaited; his fiancé was going to come, too. It was Christmas break but her dad had said she could drive up for the funeral and stay two days as long as family was there. She could look over everything and would surely agree that it was a good idea to start out with everything in the house complete. He grabbed a bowl of cereal and waited.

NO! had been the firm response. Each time he had repeated his appeal she had added another firm no to her answer. Pretty soon she had started to sound like a woodpecker going at it on a hollow tree. No no no no no no no no no no no no NO! In three days everything he hadn't packed away had been sold except he had also been able to secure the complete bedroom set he had used since childhood and the pictures in the room as well. The house was locked and he was glad to have the offer to live above a funeral home and take care of assisting there as needed. At least he wasn't homeless, but he felt very, very alone with his "little Katrina" gone.

She had helped him load his things into his car before she left. As he was driving away she saw a packet of papers that must have fallen out of one of the boxes. She picked it up and glanced at it quickly. Ah, something he wrote. I wonder what it is? I bet it will be interesting. I can give it back to him after break. She stuck it in the front seat beside her and headed home.

The young man stowed his things in the corner of his new apartment and got to work. It seemed that everyone had decided to stay alive for Christmas and then died. There was a constant rush and he was busy every minute of every day. Therapeutic, he thought. I don't have time to miss my favorite girls. God is good!

Beth arrived home and unpacked her things in her room. She had carried the packet of papers in under her arm and it had been covered by the coat she threw on her bed. Now as she finished straightening up and hung up her coat she spied it. Interesting title, she thought. I didn't know he was into westerns.

Buffalo Stampede. Maybe I won't bother with it after all. But curiosity overcame her and she peeked at the first page.

An hour later she put down the manuscript. She had been riveted to the book from page one. How did he know, she asked herself? How did he know all about her? She was disturbed and decided to reread it all. Yes, she concluded, after the second reading, it was impossible. He couldn't know any of that, but he did. A cold chill ran down her spine. I must be crazy. It's impossible and that's it.

She opened the folder to return the manuscript and noticed that she had completely overlooked another stack of papers that were also there. It was unlike the other papers which were all hand written. "Commentary – Behind the Scenes of Buffalo Stampede" was typed on the cover page. Quickly she flipped inside and it was all typed like the cover. I've come this far, she thought, I can't stop now.

As she turned each page she felt an increased tightening in her chest. The key character was unnamed, but she was named. She was the girl with the waist length brown hair and dancing green eyes playing the role of leading lady. The leading man was unnamed, but it had to be him! She had asked the question and he had answered it. He had been closer to his grandmother than anyone else. The pieces fit, but he had stopped with her death and the strange meeting in her living room. Who had he been talking to in the living room after his grandma died?

Wait a minute! Who am I talking to, she thought. I'm talking to me, but when he said it he seemed to be talking to someone else. And who was Reverend Stout? He appeared in both manuscripts. And the main character's mother, no way. She's just too nice. None of that could be true of her. Still, he was there and she was there. And whoever he was talking with had made it clear that if she knew about him she would leave them. NO! Not them. Him. She couldn't leave them. Who was "them"? She could leave him, but not "them"; who was "them"? Maybe he had been doing what his professor had told him to do back in his first year away at school. That would be weird. He had told her that just to work in their church he had to sign an agreement that he wouldn't do just about anything. Drugs was on that list and if she knew anything at all about him, then she was absolutely certain that he wouldn't do what he said he wouldn't do.

My mind is going crazy, she muttered. I have to stop this ridiculous thinking. But it didn't stop. If I am in there, and I AM in there, then he must be in there too. Who else can he be than the young man coming of age? And if he is him, then how much of what he says is true? I know he had an unhappy childhood. That part is true. He said he used to smoke. That part is true. He said he went to school and dropped out, twice, so that part is true. But does he really have all those fears? Did he really think over and over again about killing himself? Does he still? Does he just add his vivid imagination to create a more exciting character? Why am I talking to myself?

She shoved the typed manuscript into the folder with the other one. Then she thought of where it could be - the book that might have answers. Where had she put it? That was years ago. It had to be someplace. She went out into the other room.

"Mom," she called. "Do you know where the stuff is that we got on the vacation we took to trace our genealogy when I was in junior high school?"

"Probably in the basement stuffed in a box marked 'school stuff'. You can poke around in there if you want. First, though, come and tell me about your trip. Did everything go all right? You didn't have any trouble on the road did you? Letting you go by yourself was a big worry to your father and me."

Chapter 18
Sad Confirmation

What a surprise Beth had planned for her fiancé. The only thing was that she wasn't sure at all that he would like it. His manuscript had given her the idea and she knew that she could successfully explain what she was going to do without referring to his writing. Neither she nor her mother had been able to find the book she sought that she had hoped would bring some answers about his manuscript. Her mother, however, assured her she would keep looking as she was sure it had to be somewhere.

So her parents had returned her to school at the end of Christmas break and she had begun to form her plan. What her young man coming of age needed was encouragement. He needed her to be the one to bathe his wounds and pour salve in the cuts from the buffalo stampede. It was her call, as Herr Schmitt had said Katrina, to help him when he couldn't help himself. And she would. She just hoped he wouldn't be too upset when she did. She looked at the clock on her desk. He'll be here to pick me up in ten minutes, she thought, I don't want to keep him waiting. She grabbed her coat and went to the dorm entrance where he would pick her up on the way to church.

One thing he never was was late. He greeted her with a kiss and settled her into the front seat of his subcompact car. They chatted about how the rest of her vacation had gone as they took the brief drive to church. A small knot had begun to form in her stomach. What if he doesn't like what I am going to do at all? What if it gets him in trouble? What if everyone starts to think I'm crazy? Well, I guess that is just how messy it can be cleaning up the bloody wounds made by a million buffalo hooves. And so her thoughts were tossed about during most of the Sunday school hour. But at the end she had regained her focus and was ready.

Pastor Combes always ended his class with the question, does anyone have any questions? No one ever did, but she did today. She struggled to keep her hand in check until he actually asked for questions before she committed to asking hers. Then she raised it quickly before he would make the general assumption that no one did and close the class with prayer.

"Pastor, what do you think of suicide? Is it a sin?"

"I don't think you are going to find that to be a big issue among Christian people," he replied. "Perhaps some who said they were Christians might do so, but a real believer would be able to put more trust in God. Does that answer your question?"

"Not completely. What if a person were just really depressed and couldn't shake it off and then killed themself; a Christian person I mean."

"Well, I don't think you will find that a real issue among Christian people either. This sounds like some strange idea you have picked up at that public college you go to. The world wants to cover up their problems with all kinds of mumbo-jumbo that excuses every kind of behavior or thinking. You'll hear that in your classes there all the time. It's too bad you didn't go to a good Bible college where you wouldn't have heard such things. Depression is a sorry excuse the world makes for being unhappy. What they need is Jesus. Then they wouldn't be depressed. I'm sorry, but that is all the time I have for an answer right now." He prayed and dismissed the class.

The young man coming of age sat looking at her in stunned amazement and said nothing. What is he thinking, she wondered. Does he hate me already? No one else in the class stopped to talk to her as they usually did when they filed out. The young man's face remained expressionless. He turned his gaze to the empty podium and his eyes took on the same look of emptiness. She placed her hand on his arm but he remained unresponsive. Then Pastor Combes returned and placed his hand on the young man's shoulder and signaled him to follow him into the office.

"What kind of crazy question was that that she asked?" he demanded. "Have you no control over her? She still dresses like a harlot and I have warned you about that before. Now she tries to undermine me in my Sunday school class. She is going to be the ruination of your ministry, if you are even still considering the ministry."

"I don't know why she asked that question," the young man responded. "As to her clothes, if you saw the other girls on campus you would actually think she dressed modestly."

The pastor shrugged off the young man's answer. Then he continued, "As to the ministry, do you really mean to pursue it? If so, why did you take a job that makes you work on Sundays? I can't have you on staff and have you setting a bad example. The choir can't have you missing. Who will lead them on Wednesday night in practice? Who will lead them on Sunday morning? This job you have at the funeral home, if you want to keep working on staff here, you will have to quit there."

"When I came here," the young man replied with a racing heart, "you said that you would pay me as time went on. If you paid me then I could leave that job and be here."

"I did not say that I would pay you. I said that I would see about paying you if things went well. You have shown that things are not going well. I take it your answer then is that you are going to keep your job that keeps you from being here one Sunday a month and two Wednesday nights a month. Is that correct?" The young man nodded. "Then I will find a new music director and see you when you decide to come." With that he opened the office door and the young man knew he was dismissed.

He found Beth sitting in the back pew of the church. She looked very alone. His heart still stinging at his pastor's rebuke and he fell easily prey to anxiety about his fiancée as well. Was she planning to end their relationship? Was her question just a means of exposing him and then leaving him? Had she decided over vacation that she really didn't want to marry him after all and this was just her way of saying it? Silently he approached her and still in silence he helped her on with her coat and led her to the car.

"What did he say to you?" she prompted before he turned on the ignition. She raised her very sad green eyes to him and they were misty with tears. Have I really blown it, she asked herself? Have I made him so angry he doesn't want me anymore? I was so stupid to think that asking that question would help him see how much I care.

He reached slowly across the shift console and took her hand. "He said that I am a lucky man to have a girl who is not afraid to be ashamed to ask an honest question. He also said that since I have my new job that will keep me from being here every week that he will replace me as music leader." Then he exhaled slowly and started the car. "I have to get you back to campus before you miss your dinner and I have to get back to the funeral home. My shift starts at two. The post Christmas rush seems to be over and I will get some studying done. I will call you this afternoon if I can, all right?"

"Is that really what he said?"

"Would I lie to you?" He sighed. "Yes, he said that I was done as music leader."

Not wishing to press the point on what else was said she asked, "Is everything else OK?"

"Yeah. I just wondered why you asked that question. Why did you?"

"Well, it was the first question I ever asked you and you gave such an excellent answer I just wanted to see if he was as smart as you. But nobody is a smart as you." She smiled warmly.

"Nor any girl as beautiful as you," he replied and with that they found themselves at the entrance door to her dorm. "I will really try to call you this afternoon, even if I have to skip some homework. OK?" She nodded. They kissed and he let her go into the dorm.

Driving back to his apartment he asked himself over and over again why he never had the courage to tell her the things Pastor really said about her. Did he fear she would leave him if she knew of his commitment to the church and that the pastor didn't like her? Over and over he rehearsed what he should have said and how he should have phrased it. But he wasn't going to change his story now. At least she didn't tell him she was leaving him.

He prepared himself a quick lunch. It wasn't much, but he didn't need much. What he needed was the girl with the waist length brown hair and dancing green eyes. He didn't want to see them filled with tears again.

After lunch he decided that the last thing he wanted to do was study. The emotional and mental high he had been on for the past four months was fading fast. He could feel the lethargy and sorrow start to engulf him again. He had lost his home once again, but he only had one more semester to tough it out and then they could start a new home. That was, if she was not leaving him. The thought clung to him and permeated his heart and soul and mind. Damn! His mind shouted in frustration. He didn't want to fall back into the abyss. Beth would see it and then she would most certainly go. Why would she stay with such a freak show as him?

To calm his growing sense of loss he made a quick search for his writing portfolio and then considered that it had inadvertently been sent with a few of his things to his mother's house. He grabbed a new notebook and headed to the office to man the hopefully quiet desk until his shift ended at eight. Until then maybe Daniel and Katrina could have a better life than his.

Chapter 19
Summer into Autumn

The next few weeks in the new settlement of Martinsville were filled with activity. Temporary shelters were upgraded and better and safer confinement was made for the livestock. The routine that had been established on the wagon train was begun anew. Each night there was a short service, shorter than before, where Herr Schmitt led them all in Scripture reading, confessions and prayers. Sunday remained a day of rest and refreshment and church.

By common agreement it was decided that German would be the language spoken in Martinsville. Tom and Daniel were excluded from the requirement, but being immersed in it with the others every day they soon could converse in German more and more. Katrina was given permission from her father to also speak to Daniel in English and he also spoke to Daniel in English when he gave him private lessons each Wednesday night after evening prayers. But Herr Schmitt rejoiced at how quickly Daniel was able to grasp part of his lessons in German.

At the end of June those who had been designated from the beginning were sent on their way back for more supplies. After much discussion it was decided to send them to Council Bluffs instead of Missouri. It would save them nearly twenty days on the round trip and be worth any extra cost incurred in supplies. One train that had set out from Council Bluffs had already passed their settlement and assured them that quality supplies could be found there. Glad that their separation would be less long than planned the men chosen for the task set out. This time each of the eight wagons going was pulled by a team of eight horses. It reflected the intention of bringing back a great quantity of supplies to last them through the winter.

During the absence of those sent for supplies a real town began to spring up on the prairie beside the Platte River. First to be built was a Soddy barn. It was left open on the southern exposure but enclosed on three sides by sloping sod walls. A roof was made of rough cottonwood planking, supported by cottonwood rafters undergirded by cottonwood posts. The planking was then covered with extra canvas tops from the wagons and the whole thing covered with a layer of sod. It wasn't pretty, but the cattle and horses would be sheltered from winter storms. The remaining eight wagons, Tom's included, were then carefully disassembled and made into four small dwellings also given temporary roofs of Conestoga wagon canvases. The women and small children were housed in these buildings. The men made two large crude tents of the canvases and stayed in them while work was done on building more houses.

When those sent for supplies returned from Council Bluffs in mid-August there was much rejoicing. The shortened trip gave them much more time to get buildings erected than if they had gone to Missouri. Also, the prices had not been any greater than originally planned. All eight wagons had been loaded to the absolute breaking point and the eight horse teams looked spent from their labor, but they were back and safe. Rest would restore the horses and family reunions restored the men. Now five of the eight wagons were disassembled and with the new supplies a shelter was provided for each family. The smallest families, like Tom and Daniel, were given one of the original small dwellings, now with finished roofs, and others received slightly larger ones.

No other wagon trains had passed them since mid-July. From those that had come, however, they had received some household items that the settlers moving west realized by then that they couldn't continue to haul. The stresses from the trail, even just this far from Missouri, were beginning to tell on the once eager immigrants. In return for the items left behind those from Martinsville had refreshed those going by with fresh eggs and butter. A few of the men had taken a day to hunt and had returned with six buffalo pulled behind a team of horses. Much of the meat had been smoked and reserved for later use, but some was provided fresh to those still with a long way to go on their westward journey. Thus the ministrations from the community of Martinsville available to travelers heading west had become known. As those heading west reported the source of their assistance in places like Fort Laramie and other western outposts, the message was relayed back to places like Council Bluffs and Independence by traders headed east.

By the time the first killing frost came on the prairie in late September, sixteen almost finished dwellings dotted the landscape that just months before had been an empty expanse of virgin prairie. While some had worked others had continued with hunting expeditions and there was an ample supply of dried buffalo meat to sustain all the families through the long winter ahead. There were also over twenty carefully tanned buffalo hides to keep many families warm during the howling winter blizzards that lay ahead. A buffalo herd had actually set up a grazing site less than a mile from the Martinsville encampment. Several weeks after they had moved on Daniel was assigned to take a wagon of younger boys to their grazing area and collect buffalo chips. It had been a day long expedition and the boys had returned on foot as the wagon had been filled to overflowing with prairie fuel. A tent had been set up for storing them and the boys were sent on two return trips.

The killing frost was followed by two weeks of mild weather in which all the settlers redoubled their efforts to have things ready when the Indian summer would end. A second shelter had to be completed for the many horses. Prairie grass was scythed down and stacked in huge piles for winter feed for the animals. These too had to be preserved from the ravages of the coming winter weather. The boys were sent on more trips to the buffalo grazing ground and more supplies were added into storage. By early November the work was begun each morning on a landscape covered by hard frost. But on they labored knowing from stories told and retold from those who had been on the prairie before them that frozen ground, a cold northwest wind and flat gray skies were the least of the weather related problems that were still to come during their first prairie winter.

And come it did. Just before Thanksgiving the sky to the northwest had grown ever darker from morning to late afternoon. The wind had picked up into a raw and cutting gale. Then just before a dreary and invisible sunset the first hard flakes of snow began to spit from the angry sky. The work of building was over. The work of surviving had just begun.

Winds that would have sunk many a ship on the roiling ocean battered against the isolated dots on the wide prairie. Neighbors who only yesterday seemed to dwell only a few steps from one another now were separated by countless miles of blinding white. Every sliver of open space on their quickly built houses became jets of frozen air charging in to steal their warmth and security. What had seemed so tightly covered over revealed unexpected chinks in the armor of hearth and home.

Wisely the men had placed rope guidelines to the two barns. Bent double against the raging storm and feeling the piercing cold easily penetrate their warmest clothing they daily milked the cows, gathered the few eggs still being laid and kept the animals fed and the barns cleaned. Twice daily they staggered snow covered and nearly frozen into their slightly warmer dwellings and gave thanks that God was good.

After three days the blizzard had exhausted its fury and the brilliant sun, radiant but cold, again appeared in the sky. The men gathered in the cow barn to assess what damage had been done. All were alive, men and beasts, and a prayer of thanksgiving ascended to the Father of life. Every home still stood, some with more small piles of snow inside than others, but they all stood. A prayer of thanksgiving was offered to God the Mighty Fortress. The supply tent housing the prairie fuel had blown in on the supplies it contained, but the supplies themselves were intact. A prayer of thanksgiving ascended to the God who supplies the daily bread and means to fix it. Tomorrow would be the Sabbath day. Today everything that needed to be fixed must be fixed. With a prayer for strength in their endeavors the men set out to do their work in the cold frozen white land they now lived in.

Daniel was impressed at just how thankful everyone was. He hadn't seen Katrina for three days and he wasn't sure just how thankful he was about that. He agreed with them all, however, that their sheer survival at all was a most amazing and God blessed situation. He would pull his weight with the other men and work to make their survival more probable.

But Daniel had also noted that he had begun to think again of the big bull buffalo. He had seen him at the edge of his dream as he awoke each morning. But the old buffalo was doing more than that. He had stopped chewing his cud and was leading his herd on a merry romp over Daniel's mind. Did Katrina know his increasing fear? Could he tell it to Tom? There were so many more urgent things to handle than his sissy mind. Lives were at stake if they became distracted. He could not distract them. It would be a sin against the community to impose his creeping pain into the other things that must absolutely be done. But he couldn't keep his creeping pain from his own mind. The bright sun that the others looked at rejoicing was for him obscured with a dismal gray cloud. The howling wind had stopped but the howling gale in his mind had just begun to blow. His eyes followed the men as they trudged out in the cold snow to do what must be done. Then his eyes shifted to the sharp hoof cleaning knife hanging on the wall. He was certain; then and there certain, that he would be less of a distraction if he were dead.

Chapter 20
Skirting the Issue

The young man coming of age slammed his pen down on the desk with such vehemence that it would have woken the dead if any such temporary residents were occupying rooms there that weekend. That's not where I expected to end up, his mind shouted, and the words echoed from neuron to neuron until the sound slowly died. Daniel was supposed to help me out. Where's the light and love from the guy when I need it? I'd call him a fair weather friend, but he seems to be having a little run of bad weather of his own.

He looked out the office window at the mountain of snow piled up nearly twelve feet tall at the end of the funeral home parking lot. He sighed; at least we didn't get all ours in one blast. He flipped the page in his notebook and began writing an essay on comparative psychological theories. It made more sense today than Daniel. Then he angrily drew a large X across the page. Psychology, the subject that Pastor had so disparaged this morning, was the young man's major. He was even working on a grant proposal for further research on a project he had supervised which apparently disproved given assumptions on haptic perceptions. OK, so it wasn't the grandest work ever done and it wouldn't get him further in his ministry goals, but it was a successful study.

Beautiful green eyes had been proud of him. That was nice, very nice. The thought relieved some of his stress. Maybe it was a good thing she asked that question this morning. He began to consider how it had revealed the reality of a modern Reverend Stout. He had witnessed all the pain Stout had brought to Daniel. Now he was protecting the same man's name and honor from Beth knowing the truth. Who did he love more? What a question! Or was he just being mercenary? Pastor was a step to future ministry and it was best to cultivate instead of plow under such opportunities. But that would be equally loathsome, he thought. Choosing filthy lucre over honesty with his beloved, what kind of relationship was that? Maybe she should break up with him if that were his true motive. True motives? Did anybody really have them? Aren't we all just self seeking sinners after all? I certainly stand condemned of uncertainty, he concluded, and turned a new page to finish his essay.

Work done he checked the time. It was only three o'clock. I could use some cheering up, he assured himself of at least one true motive. He did need cheering up. Making sure the incoming line was still available he called his lady love.

"Hi," came the bright response. "Did you get all your studying done so quickly?"

"Not all of it. I did finish one essay for Psych Theory. It will be an essay of pure genius if I got the right names with the right theories. There are so many of them and they split such fine hairs that I lose track. I left my book upstairs and I can't leave the desk. If my memory serves me well, though, I did get them right. How about you? Doing any studying or just laying around in your PJ's and vegging out?"

"Unlike you, I haven't been given an assignment yet. Why do you have work to do anyway? We just got back from break."

"The syllabus laid out what assignments we will be doing and I am getting a start. For this class the syllabus came with the book at the bookstore. Since I want to spend as much time as possible with you, I thought I would get a head start. I seemed to feel more energetic when I bought the book, but I am pressing on with the work anyway."

That was a good believable lie, he told himself. Maybe even it was a good half truth. He knew his real motive was to get as much work as he could do done before the crash in his mind hit critical mass. He could salvage what he could of his assignments by getting them done early.

"Is my baby feeling down?" She repeated for the third time and disrupting his thoughts.

"Oh, yeah, a little. Well, give me twenty years and I will recover from my grandmother's death. That's point A. Point B would be this morning. I do understand not being able to continue as music director. Someone who is always available is really necessary. It's just the abrupt way he did it that irks me. But you saw in class today at the end of his answer to your question that he can be abrupt. Speaking of this morning, why did you really ask that question?"

"If I said I did it for you, what would you think? I know everything has gotten you upset lately. I understand, at least as much as I can, how sad you are about your grandmother. Maybe I just wanted you to see how much you really know and how much you will really be able to help people. As to the other stuff, don't let it get you down. I still have the best answer anyone could give me and it came from you. Did you . . ." Suddenly she remembered that if she finished her question he would know she had read his manuscript.

"Did I what?"

"Did you ever begin a thought and forget where it was going before you finished it?" She quickly covered her near mistake. "Do you have a brilliant psychological theory about that?"

"Well, actually yes, to both questions. The reason is competitive cognitive interference. We have two things on our mind and they kind of chase each other around and both get lost."

"Did you just make that up?"

"Yes. But it sounds good, doesn't it? Now let me guess what your second thought was so that I can reinforce it in your mind. You were thinking how much more you would actually rather be here and having me hold you tight and smothering you with kisses than be talking on the phone? Right?"

"Don't get ideas, Big Boy. You'll get us both excommunicated."

"You were just supposed to say yes and make me feel good."

"Then yes, but don't get any ideas."

"I always have ideas when I talk to you."

"Most of which will have to wait, I'm sure."

"Not if you'll marry me tomorrow."

"We're getting married in May after you graduate, and that's final," she laughed.

"For sure and true?"

"For absolute positive cross my heart and hope to die, stick a needle in my eye sure and true. Yes. Although my parents did again try to talk me out of it. 'O honey, they said, why do you want to marry a poor teacher or even poorer preacher? Wait a few years and Rodney, remember him, he always liked you, will graduate from dental school and you can have anything you want. In the meantime you can finish your schooling, too.' I told them you were what I want and they sighed and we looked at pictures of wedding dresses. But Mom is going to make me one. It is beautiful. In only five months you can see it."

Cheered by her assurances that they were not breaking up he sighed with deep relief. "Is your roommate back yet?"

"She got back an hour ago. She's down the hall talking to somebody. Most everyone is back in dorm now. Half of them have paraded into my room to look at my ring. They're all jealous, jealous, jealous. I got the good one."

If only she knew the truth, he thought, then she wouldn't be so sure. "Well it takes the good one to know one, I guess. Well, I do have more work to get ahead on. I'll call you after eight. Love you. Bye."

Relaxed and at least less depressed by his fears, if not the darkness in his brain, he got back to work. Before eight o'clock rolled around he had finished three more essays and rough drafted a paper on cognitive theory. It's good I like to write, he thought. If all classes were writing classes I could finish school in a couple weeks and we could get married right away. But, alas, they aren't all writing classes and I must grunt it out for five more months. If it weren't so unethical I would love to earn some extra money and write papers for other students.

Maybe I should focus on trying to write a book. Only problem is I would be too intimidated to send it to a publisher and it would just sit with everything else in my portfolio. I do hope that it didn't get lost in the move. I could write Mom and ask her to find it. Or not. What if she read it when she did? That would be bad. As far as she is concerned I am the brilliant child without problems. I would really hate to burst her bubble.

There's an idea. I could have Daniel and Katrina burst Herr Schmitt's bubble. I could have Katrina come running into the barn just as he places the knife on his wrist. She would cry out, "No, Daniel, no! I love you." Then he would grab her and smother her smooth lips with passionate kisses. Herr Schmitt would return to the barn to see where he was and find them in passionate embrace. He would insist that they now get married immediately. And they all lived happily ever after. I wish! I should stop the folly of my dreams, he concluded, close up the office, get something to eat and call my sweetie back.

Chapter 21
Truth or Consequences

The beautiful young girl with the waist length brown hair turned her tear stained green eyes into her pillow and cried softly. She had just placed the phone back in its cradle after having her second talk of the day with the young man. "I love you, too," she had said. And she meant it. Then why, her heart cried, do I always lie to him and let him lie to me? I know he loves me, but I know he isn't being honest with me. I know I love him, too, but I am hiding something really important from him. Is this how we will always be? If we can't be really honest now, will we ever be honest?

"Is everything all right?" her roommate asked with concern.

"Oh, yes. I just love him so much that sometimes it makes me cry with happiness." There I go again, she thought. I can't be honest with anyone. If I told Julie and she let it slip to someone else then how far would it go before it got back to him? That's it again. It's not being honest with him. Can we really get married like this? Softly crying she fell into a restless sleep.

When the alarm rang at six she was already up and had firmly determined to have things out with him today. She would order an extra large sack lunch from the dorm cafeteria and they could eat it together in the student union. He didn't usually have a lunch. She knew it was because he had no money, but he always just said, "I really don't need much," and again she didn't press him. Her resolve weakened. Maybe some things were better not pressed. There was an honest point of pride that should be respected. She respected it with his income, why couldn't she respect it with his emotions?

She realized that the answer was simple. She did know about his finances. She just didn't throw them up in his face every day. He knew that she knew and she knew that when she could get an extra large sack lunch he really appreciated having something to eat. She could do that without having to say a word to him. It was because he knew that she knew that he could accept the help she could give. So it wasn't a secret between them. Only what she had done by reading his manuscript and he what he had done by not telling her how depressed he really was, those were big lies and big secrets. Again confirmed in her determination to open things up she went to breakfast and ordered the lunch.

They found a booth in the union in an area where no one else was sitting. After they had finished eating while idly chatting about small things she decided to take the plunge. She reached her hands across the table and took both of his into hers. "Darling," she was amazed at that word. She had certainly never used it before, but it did sound kind of nice. "I think there are things that we are not being fully honest about with each other. Marriage is based on honesty; don't you agree?"

"Yes, of course," he answered while a cold chill filled his whole being. What is she going after, he wondered? She's been fishing for something since she got back from break. Smiling with his lips, but not with his heart, he added, "Go on."

"Do you think it is good to keep secrets from each other?"

"Might there not be some things that are so irrelevant that the secret need not be shared? I wet my bed until I was ten or some such thing?"

"Certainly in some ways we will never be able to know each other fully. Too much happens and has happened in life to know it all. If you wet the bed until you were ten, that isn't exactly the kind of secret that could undermine a relationship, is it? And did you?" she laughed.

"No to both of those questions. Do you have something you want to get off your chest that you think might impair our relationship? I love you and it won't. If you didn't tell me then I would never know and it wouldn't impair our relationship that way either."

"Well, what if it somehow came out later and you became so angry at the lie and secret that had been hidden so long that you couldn't come to grips with it? What then?"

"You've been acting strange since you got back. What is the matter? Are you trying to break up with me softly?"

"No!" she exclaimed. "I told you last night that I am cross my heart hope to die going to marry you. I meant it."

"All right, my beautiful one, we will swap secrets. You go first."

A sudden panic seized her. He had not taken any of what she had said seriously, or maybe he did and just didn't want to tell her his secret. Where is Herr Schmitt when I need him, she asked herself dejectedly. Now what was she going to say? Was she going to tell him what she had done and have him storm off or be so broken that he would slink off and never come back? Did she want to see him broken? No! She wanted to help him; care for him; love him into happiness. If she spilled her secret when he didn't seem to care about the seriousness of what she was saying, how would he react?

"Come on, O love of my life," give it up. "What is your secret? Then I will tell you mine."

Her heart pounded and her hands were sweating. She hoped he hadn't noticed but pulled them back just in case. "You always say you love my 'virgin lips'. Well, they aren't. I was really popular in high school, you know, and I had a lot of dates." It was all true but it was a lie of the devil and she could hardly finish. Her heart was throbbing in her throat, choking off the words. "Well, I found out that I liked kissing and so I did it a lot. You are not the first one to kiss these 'virgin lips'." Her eyes were streaming with tears and she alone knew it wasn't because of the stupidity of her confession but because she had utterly failed to be honest.

The young man stared at her with incredulity. So much choking emotion for such a small matter; how he did love her. But the whole scene seemed so farcical that he could not control the emotion of extreme humor that he saw in that confession. Suddenly he burst out in uproarious laughter. Heads all over the Union turned in their direction. Trying to choke himself back to sobriety he panted, "Oh, how I do love you. You are a treasure of fine diamonds. They will always be virgin lips to me," then he collapsed on his arms which rested on the table and laughed until his body shook the booth.

A sharply vicious kick to his shins arrested his reverie. "I'm serious," she pouted, now growing angry at both her dishonesty and his response. "I suppose you have nothing to confess."

He looked up and dried the tears of mirth that streaked his face. "You've topped anything that I could say," he choked out still trying to suppress another laughing fit.

"How about Carolyn?" She snapped and then wanted to bite off her tongue. How could I have said that?! How could I have been so mean? Now he will think that this was all just a sorry excuse for me to pry something from him that I don't care about. I am so, so stupid.

The young man no longer laughed. His stare was steely, but behind the iron of his eyes she saw the hurt of love destroyed. "So this is what it has been all about."

"No! No!" she stammered. "I don't know why I said that. I am so sorry."

But the damage was done. He should have told her before. Why, he wasn't sure, but it was obvious he should have. Who could have told her was his question.

"I didn't mean to say it," she pleaded. "I was just so angry at you laughing at me. It means nothing to me. Forgive me."

"I should have told you. It is just that it was a long time ago. It was in my old life which I would rather forget. I'm sorry it hurt you."

"No, it didn't. I don't care. It is your old life and that is dead. I just got so angry for no good reason. What I said about my 'virgin lips' did sound really stupid and probably really funny. I do think we do have secrets, though, and I think we should work more on honesty on being open. I just made up that stupid story, well not made it up because it is true, but made it up right then because I am afraid for no good reason to tell you the truth.

"You're wondering how I know, don't you? I know you are. When we went to see your friend Steve last fall he told me. I didn't care then and he was upset, I think, that I didn't. I never thought about it again until just now and out it came."

"Well, I told Steve the story as a confession. You know, confess your sins one to another. He was my confessor and as such he should have kept it a secret. I should have told you."

While they reached their hands across the table they both thought to themselves; what kind of foolish play are we living? I need to tell her/him the truth, but I can't. Suddenly he saw himself beside her. You're right, Bozo, the other sneered, you can't. She might forgive Carolyn but she would never understand or accept the truth about who we are. The young man agreed.

In the darkness of his room that night the young man's sleep was suddenly disturbed. A second time he felt something shove against his foot. Switching on the light he saw what couldn't be seen and drew in his breath sharply. "Daniel?" he asked with a quiver in his voice.

"Yes, I'm glad you recognize me. You seemed to have left me in a precarious position. I know that it is really where I left you, but we both need to get out of it. We need to do it for both your sake and mine. We need to do it now."

The young man looked at the clock. 2AM. "Now?"

"Do you really think you can put it off any longer? If you do you will end up where we left me." Get out your notebook and get things settled. It really is now or never.

Chapter 22
Opening

Daniel's eyes were riveted on the knife. Everything else disappeared from his vision. Trancelike he walked to the tool of his destruction. "It's better this way. It's better this way," sang the siren song which had filled his ears to overflowing. No other sound could penetrate and no other sight could distract his eyes. He grabbed the hilt of the knife and began to lift its leather strap over the peg on which it hung as the song now spilled from his own lips.

A steel hand clasped his wrist. An iron vise squeezed until he had dropped his weapon. "How," he suddenly heard the iron voice of Herr Schmitt barking sharp German words in his ear, "how can you say 'it's better this way', Daniel? For whom is it better? Is it better for me to fail you as I failed Philip? Is it? Is it better for Katrina to feel for the rest of her life that she failed to protect the one she loves? Is it? Is it better for Herr Miller to lose you after losing his wife? Is it? Is it better for the men who would have to stop fixing the damage from the storm to dig a hole to put you in and leave their families cold and in danger? Is it? Is it better for you to miss the love of a good woman and a life of service to your God? Is it?"

The stinging reality of each question left Daniel shaking. Every word Herr Schmitt said was absolutely true. But Daniel had felt so overwhelmed. The buffalo had been stampeding him for over a week. He must try to explain it to Herr Schmitt. He couldn't take the pounding hooves anymore. All that he had seen that morning, all the damage, even though it was all repairable had been one hoof too many.

"Herr Schmitt," he cried, tears streaking down his face and freezing in the scruff of his beard, "Herr Schmitt, I just couldn't take anymore hooves."

"So the bull buffalo has called his herd to a stampede, has he? Did he do it during the storm? Did he start it this morning as you looked at all the damage done?"

"Almost a week ago, sir. At first they just sort of walked toward me and I tried to run. But then they walked faster and I tried to run faster. They started to trot and I couldn't run anymore. I fell down and they just started to walk slowly over me. Each heavy hoof dug into me with searing pain. All through the storm they just kept on walking, crushing me further and further into the ground. Last night they started to trot and then this morning they started in a race to see which of them could finish me off."

"So, Daniel, he started it a week ago. Did you tell Katrina? Did you tell Herr Miller? Did you tell me when we sat together and studied the catechism? Would Katrina have prayed for you? Would Herr Miller have prayed for you and held you securely in his arms? Did you think that I would not understand?"

Daniel hung his head. Yes, everyone cared, but he had been ashamed that he couldn't stand against the pain on his own. He was afraid that everyone would have thought he had little faith. Certainly a man of faith did not have these pains, these fears, these horrors in his mind. Certainly a man of faith could overcome them by his own prayers. But he hadn't. He had failed in his prayers and the stampede had grown worse. Certainly he wasn't a man of faith.

"Shouldn't I just be able to rely on God?" he asked petulantly.

"Daniel, what is the third portion of the Apostles' Creed?"

"I believe in the Holy Ghost, the holy Christian Church, the communion of saints, the forgiveness of sin, the resurrection of the body and the life everlasting. Can't I just rely on the Holy Ghost to help me then?"

"Does the Holy Ghost live only in you, Daniel? Does Christ live only in you?"

"No, He lives in the Church."

"Are you one with Christ and the Church and the Holy Ghost, Daniel?"

"Yes," he replied beginning to gain his composure.

"Then if you are one with them you are relying on yourself when you rely on them. Isn't that right? That, Daniel, is the communion of the saints. God made us part of each other. We need the Church."

"But what about my faith? Isn't that good enough? Shouldn't my faith be strong enough to fight off the devil?"

"When Jesus sent out the Disciples, Daniel, He sent them out two by two. Solomon said that a chord of three is not easily broken. If you got lost on this great prairie and were all alone then God would give you all you needed to stand alone. But you are not, Daniel. You live in our Christian community. God does not call you to stand alone against the devil when He has provided you help to stand."

"Then I haven't failed."

"No, Daniel, you have failed. You have failed to rely on those who you know love you. You have failed to follow the hope that I gave you when I told you my story. You have failed to do what is right by Katrina when you did not ask her help in prayer. You failed in many ways, Daniel, but the good God has preserved you."

"I have sinned, Herr Schmitt."

"And in the Name of the Father and of the Son and of the Holy Ghost I declare unto you the absolution of your sins as you come in true repentance and faith. Now there is much work to be done. I want you to take supplies of buffalo chips to every house. If they have no fire left in their stoves then I want you to rekindle them so everyone can stay warm. Go first to my house and offer your confession to Katrina. You have been absolved, but she needs to hear of your need. Now go and go quickly. It is getting very cold."

Daniel hurried to his cabin and got the canvas bag he had made. It was large enough to hold many buffalo chips. It would only take him a few trips to get what he needed for everyone. He also reached into his storage box and retrieved the two things most dear to him and placed them in the bottom of his bag. Then he slogged his way through the thigh deep snow to the supply tent. Brushing and pulling away the snow that held down the corner of the fallen tent he reached in and retrieved a dozen chips.

Frau Schmitt opened the door to him. "Come in, Daniel. What do you have in your bag?"

Daniel opened the bag and produced five chips. He went to the stove and pulled open the door. A small flame still burned without emitting enough heat to even keep the stove hot to the touch. Carefully he placed a chip near the flame and blew gently. As it too caught on fire he added two more and closed the door. "It will start to get warm soon. After awhile you can put the other two in and I will be back with more before today is over." He turned toward the door and came face to face with Katrina and Philip.

Daniel swallowed hard, but he must believe in the Holy Christian Church and the communion of the saints. Standing back so that he could also see Frau Schmitt as he spoke he began slowly. "First, I want to ask you, Philip, if you are old enough to be relied on to keep a secret?" Philip nodded eagerly. "I have a secret, Philip, which only a few people know. I don't know if Herr Schmitt has even told you, Frau Schmitt, but I will tell you now. Sometimes I get very sad for no apparent reason. The sadness may last for many days or weeks. Sometimes it leaves me very tired and sometimes very afraid, but I never seem to know of what. Sometimes I get so sad and so afraid that I want to hurt myself. I may even want to kill myself."

Tears ran down Katrina's and Frau Schmitt's faces while Philip stood wide eyed and spellbound. "When a person in the church hurts, Philip, they should call on others to pray for them and encourage them. I haven't been doing that. I have felt very sad and very much like hurting myself for many days now. This morning when I was in the barn I nearly took the hoof cleaning knife and killed myself. Your father, Philip, stopped me. He saved my life.

But, I should have told him how I felt many days before the storm hit. I should have told Katrina as well. I should have asked for their prayers and accepted their kind words of love and assurance, but I did not. So now I tell you all this story and ask your forgiveness." They all silently nodded.

"I have also brought something for you Katrina. It is the two things that matter most to me beside you." He reached in his bag and pulled out his half eagle coin and pitted knife. The one is what I have to give you to start our life together. The other is what I give you in pledge not to use it but to rely on your prayers and love to help me through my times of depression. Now I must make sure all the families are warm."

Again he pushed out into the freezing air, but he felt wonderfully warmed inside. Pressing his weight against the well formed drifts he continued his rounds to each home. When every fire was lit he returned to each home until they were all well supplied with fuel to keep them through the coming Sabbath day.

He ended where he began and accepted a cup of hot coffee from Katrina. Frau Schmitt brought him a piece of heavily buttered bread. "You will make my Katrina a fine husband, Daniel. It took true manly courage to tell us all, including Philip, how you feel. If you always be this honest with her she will always be a strength and support to help you in life."

Katrina took a chair beside him and held his hand. "Just a wink, Daniel, will let me know of your need. You don't have to say all those hard things all the time. Just give me a wink and I will know. All our life, Daniel, I will know. I will help to hold you up. Ich liebe dich."

Chapter 23
Consensus

The young man looked up from his notebook. Daniel had moved to a sitting position but still had residence in the corner. "Good work," Daniel stated flatly. "A job well done. All is well and I thank you." His voice took on a more genial tone.

"You haven't even seen what I wrote."

"You don't think I don't know what you wrote, do you?"

"Well, then I do hope you are really happy. The outcome seems very beneficial on your side of things."

"And on your side?" Daniel asked sincerely. "Can't it be beneficial there as well?"

The young man looked around the room to see if he would find himself standing somewhere unexpectedly. "What kind of ending do you want for yourself, Daniel?"

"I want to live happily ever after, don't you?"

"Is there a happily ever after?"

"You write the script. How have you made it work for Katrina and me?"

"Just the way you wanted it. Everybody understands and all goes well."

"Why don't you try writing your script the same way? Nobody can understand what they don't know. You have pushed that theme my way repeatedly. Practice what you preach. Will Beth be happier without you? Isn't that how you had Herr Schmitt confront me? Why did you have him say that if you didn't think it was true? Will she think if you walk away into sad oblivion that she has failed at true love? What about the people you want to help heal through the Gospel? You wrote Herr Schmitt's script. Was it phony? You still have two hours until dawn. Don't let this day fail you, dear friend. I will look forward to how you write my lines when this day is over. Good night." Daniel tucked his head on his chest and seemed to go to sleep. The young man rolled over and tried to do the same but sleep wouldn't come. He rolled back to ask Daniel one more question, but Daniel was gone.

Never prone to early rising the young man never-the-less found himself wide awake by six am. It was impossible, he told himself, that he could feel so refreshed after only two hours sleep. Or had he really had a full eight hours and just one crazy dream. Beside his bed lay his notebook and reaching for it he saw that there was indeed another chapter written.

This had to be it then. This then had to be the day. If he didn't seize the courage to do it today he doubted he would ever get another chance. Three short months ago he had been convinced that it was necessary to come to a clear understanding of their future. They had both come to the same conclusion at the same time. That had clearly seemed such a divinely led confirmation that it would hold them a lifetime. Now he knew that her need for a consensus on a fully honest relationship was as necessary to her as confirmation of their future had been to him. He hoped he had not blown it yesterday when she had seemed ready and he had laughed her off. She had been ready but he hadn't; would the opportunity come again? Dressing in something less wrinkled than most of his other clothes he grabbed a quick breakfast and read his Bible until it was time to go to class.

Beth had again cried herself to sleep. Over and over in an unending loop she saw her young man reaching under his pillow for the knife she imagined he still kept there. Each time she woke up in a terrified sweat and then fell back to sleep in utter exhaustion and saw it again and again. Finally Julie shook her roommate and made sure she was completely awake. She went to the bathroom and brought her back a glass of cold water. "Now, go to sleep," she demanded. "I want to get some myself."

Again Beth slipped off into dreamland and her dream moved forward a few frames in the film. Now he was pressing the knife to his wrists. She stared in horror and he smiled at her and looked down at the knife. Inscribed on the blade was one word – honesty. Then the picture faded, but not with the expectation of the viewer that the young man had actually hurt himself. She drifted into a deeper more refreshing sleep.

"What was your problem last night?" Julie asked.

"I broke a promise to myself yesterday and it left me upset. I could see the pain it caused over and over in my dreams. Today I will keep it no matter what happens."

"If every love affair is as happy as yours, I'm glad I don't have a boyfriend."

"Bumps make life exciting, don't ya know?" the young girl laughed. She actually felt almost exuberant.

"You do realize that lack of sleep makes you weird. Right?" Laughing together they went to breakfast.

Again she had an extra large sack for lunch and again they settled in a quiet corner of the Union. After he prayed the young man began resolutely, "Do you remember last fall when we both had the same confirming experience of our relationship in the same night? Well, I don't know how you slept, but I woke up this morning with the firm conviction that we need to settle what you started yesterday."

"I hope," she replied anxiously, "that we are both going to be talking about the same thing. I woke up this morning wanting to clarify and finish what I started yesterday as well."

"Last fall I let you go first, so I get to go first this time. I may be way off base from what you had in mind, but there is something I have to tell you. I won't even hold you to your promise if you want to break it, but you must know."

She stared with anticipation into his firm gaze and replied. "I have the same need to confess something to you and if you leave me, I will understand. But if you leave, please take care of yourself and find someone else to take good care of you. Please."

Her gaze wavered from his and she bowed her head quietly and slow tears ran down her cheeks. Seeing her fears painted in the prisms of her tears he hesitated to continue. He again appeared next to her and stared in anger at himself. You're right to wait. Better not to say a word. She will never understand. I don't know about you but I love her and I don't want to lose her.

"Shut up!" he nearly shouted.

"What did you say?" she looked up at him and the tears of hurt turned to tears of anger.

"I have a bad habit of speaking to myself. I'm sorry. Sometimes the conversations erupt out loud. Talk about getting weird looks, they often come my way. Anyway, I was having a little argument with myself, really whacko, I know, but I just wanted my thoughts to shut up so I could tell you something that is very, very important.

"First and foremost I love you. Secondly, I have not lied to you; I have just neglected to tell you something that is key to who I am." His heart pounded and he gripped the table to stop the shaking of his hands. "I have unusual thoughts. It is very hard for me to express them to you or anyone. In fact, I have never told anyone but you right now how defectively my brain works. I guess on second thought I did lie to you on Sunday afternoon. It was both the truth and a lie. That is how whacked my mind works. I am doing my work ahead of time so that I can get as much done as I can before my brain energy decides to take a vacation with my emotional stability to Drearyville. The thinking stays, it just is listless and lonely.

"It rains every day in Drearyville. All the roads are full of potholes and all the flowers are dead on their stems. But that won't be their last stop. They will go on to Graveburg and lurk in the shadows of mausoleums for a while. Then they will suggest I join them there for a permanent vacation. It will take all my strength to resist their request and I will be too worn out to do as much work as I need to do to get all my courses done for graduation.

"Sometimes they take short vacations and sometimes long ones. I never know how long they will be gone. While they are in Drearyville I am emotionally flat. When they move on to Graveburg I am emotionally weary. I'm needy and the smallest rebuff can feel like the hardest slap in the face. I can be temperamental and irritable and very fearful. If I feel secure then I do better, but even then I struggle. I have failed at going away to college twice because I needed a place to feel secure in order to survive. When those times come and I am in a secure place, like home, then the landing is much softer and the emotional crash is not nearly so jarring. But it still comes and still stays. I went to my mother's the first two times, but she had no university and Grandma did. So I came here and Grandma provided that and now she is gone. I have been on the high path of having both my brain energy and emotions working well and in harmony. Those periods also vary in time and cannot be predicted. I can feel them packing their bags now and getting ready to drive to the airport. I am going to crash. I so hoped it would be soft, but now I don't know. If it's hard you won't like who I am. That's all I can say. OK, now it's your turn."

The young girl's lip quivered as she lifted her tear stained face to look him fully in the eye. "Ich liebe dich." He slumped in his seat and audibly sucked in air. "I'll say it again. Ich liebe dich. Yes, you can see that I have read your book. It fell out of one of your boxes as you were loading your car. As you drove away I found it on the ground. I read it. I read them both. I'm so sorry. They were private. But I am just a curious girl and I thought you probably wrote some really nice things so I read them. I know all about you. I Don't Care! Ich liebe dich! Can you forgive me? Can you still love me?"

"You really don't care?" he choked. "Really?"

"I care about you. I will help to hold you up. Ich liebe dich."

"How could you know that?"

"Know what?"

"Those were the last words that Katrina promised Daniel in the chapter I finished just last night. The exact words."

"I guess we green eyed girls just know how to love our men, and I do love you. I will be with you and help you have a soft landing. I promise, cross my heart and hope to die, stick a needle my eye, promise. I think we have come to the real desire I had yesterday. Now we can move forward with nothing between us.

Before we eat I have one question, - how can I help you and hold you up?"

The young man sat silently thinking for a few minutes and then answered. "I think maybe there are three ways, but they won't always be simple ways. First, be there. Depression, despair, loneliness and anxiety don't hit at scheduled times. When they hit I will need you more than usual. Be there. Second, please be patient. Don't push. I don't like change and I don't do most things quickly. Both things give me a lot of anxiety unless I am flying high mentally and emotionally. Thirdly, you can keep doing what you are really good at. Stay strong in the Lord because my problems will not always come easily on either of us. Be content with God because sometimes He will be all you have. Not much of a bargain, is it?"

"I'll take that bargain if you come along with it. We know that God has called us together to serve Him as He wants. We settled that last fall. Together, whatever your needs are, we will do it. That is settled now as well. I know who you are and what you need, at least sort of, so now we can work the rest of it out together. Now, let's eat. I'm hungry for the first time today."

Chapter 24
Not So Well Laid Plans

It was a rare treat that only came once a month. The young man had the entire weekend off lasting from Thursday night until he pulled another shift on Monday afternoon. Freed from responsibility at both church and work he had decided to take Beth home for the weekend. His mother lived only minutes from her parents but they lived in different cities. They could both spend a relaxing weekend at home and even more importantly spend seven hours round trip alone in the car together. That time, he hoped, could soothe his downward spiraling emotions.

Once free of the university and city traffic Beth pulled a notebook from her bag and said, "We have both been so busy that we haven't had a chance to do any serious discussions about a lot of things lately. I've had some things I wanted to talk to you about, but we just haven't been able to get to it. I thought now would be a good time."

The young man looked at her with slight annoyance. "What kinds of questions require you to write them down?"

"I didn't want to forget anything and I do want your serious answers and undivided attention."

"I can guarantee you my undivided attention. I'm exhausted from serious, but I'll try."

"OK. This one comes from your book. I can't believe your mother was a drug addict. Was that just for effect in the story?"

"That wasn't in the story. That was in the background. So, yes, it's true. But in all fairness to you and my mother, I really would like to clarify that issue. It wasn't like drugs most people think of as drugs. She was addicted to prescription meds. The doctor gave her uppers to get some zing in the morning to go to work. Then he gave her downers to wind down after work. All those drugs are addictive. But he gave her more and more.

"She was a perfectionist. No spot of dust could survive in our house. She was also a perfectionist as a teacher. She went in early to make sure everything was not just ready, but perfectly ready for the day. She stayed late to get her work done and not bring it home. Then she came home and fixed a big meal each night and then cleaned house before going to bed. She got little sleep and at first the pills were just a little pick-me-up. Then she would need two to get through the day, then three. By that time the pills would keep her running in high gear too late into the night so she got pills to relax and then more to relax. One day she made a mistake and apparently took her downers instead of uppers and tried to drive to work. Boom and crash. That was her addiction." He exhaled with some frustration.

"Sorry," she reached across and held his arm. "I really am, but I just had to know."

"It was a fair question. I just don't like answering it generally, but for you it was OK."

"Now question number two, and don't get upset."

He interrupted her and shook his head. "That is a bad lead-in to a question. You get the person defensive before they hear it and may get a not too honest or kind answer. Do you think I will really get upset?"

"I hope not, but I just don't know." She waited but he remained silent so she continued. "Now that you know how Pastor feels about how you are - " The young man smacked the steering wheel with his palm. Startled she broke off her question.

"You can use the word, Beth. I won't break if you say depression." His voice was tinged with sarcasm. "I won't break if you use the word suicidal. I'm sorry if I sound nasty, but they are real things. You will have to call them that all the rest of your life. They are not nasty words."

"I am sorry, really. We just have never used them and they sound so, I don't know, they just sound so not like you. They really are words that Pastor doesn't like either."

"You're right. I'm sorry I snapped. Please remember they are OK words to use." His warm smile reassured her.

Satisfied and calmer she continued. "Since Pastor Combes doesn't believe in depression as a real disease or suicide as anything short of serious or a total lack of faith, are we still going to keep going to church there?"

The young man puffed out his cheeks and exhaled slowly. "I think so, at least until graduation. He is a good preacher. We may have to look far and wide for a church that doesn't feel that way." He glanced at her open mouth and pre-empted what he suspected she was going to say. "We're not Lutherans. I had one real friend in high school and he was Lutheran. He was the most cynical God denying person you could ever meet. He'll be in the wedding so you will get to meet him. You talk about your Lutheran friends from high school like they were no better than my friend. You grew up Presbyterian and said your pastor talked about the Bible not even being true. A hundred years ago the Presbyterians were sound fundamental Bible believers. See what happened to them in a hundred years. Daniel lives in the past." Then stopping to assess the surprise on her face he concluded, "That's what you were going to suggest, right?"

She nodded. "You're right about my church and you're right about my friends. If I hadn't met a Baptist friend in junior high I never would have heard a salvation message or been saved. But I didn't know then that I would fall in love with you and that we would need a church that wasn't going to beat on you for your depression, either."

"Point taken, but I don't want to be searching around with just a few months to go. Searching means change and I hate change, especially now that I am crashing."

"There's just one more we really need to discuss."

"And you want to say, I hope it doesn't upset you, but you aren't going to say it."

"Yes," she laughed, "that's true. But here we go." Beth took a deep breath, looked out the corner of her eye at her fiancé and debated whether to ask her question or not. She took another deep breath and felt her heart pounding. He had told her to be patient. He had told her not to push. That was how she could help him, but she didn't really think this was pushing.

"Darling, I love that word since our little talk. I think I will learn to say it like an actress. Dahrrlingg! How's that?"

"Hollywood here she comes. I guess it's goodbye to me when the bright lights shine."

She smacked his shoulder. "This is serious. We have talked all about long range plans for the future of our life, but we don't even know what you are going to be doing after graduation in four months." She folded her hands in her lap and looked at him seriously. "Do you realize that?"

He stared glumly down the highway and slowly nodded his head.

"So, you have thought about this?"

"I try not to, actually. That may sound strange, but I just don't like upsetting myself that much. It may not look like it to you or to people at church or others in the classroom, but I am depressed. I'm not just depressed about our future, or lack of it, but just because I am. Last fall I was on a high. The darkness had bid me farewell for a while. You filled my days with sunshine so brightly that it was hard to imagine I had ever been depressed. It was a bad memory. But then it came back and I tried to fight it, am trying to fight it, but I am losing. You have been a huge help in fighting it, but I am still losing. I am falling. Imagine that I am a skydiver. I have bailed out of the plane and am free falling from a mile high. The earth is spinning below me as I spin in the air. Everything is a fast moving blur and I need to pull the ripcord to slow my fall and see where I am supposed to land. But, O dear one that I love beyond description, I seem to have left the parachute in the plane.

"This is all happening in dream sequence, slow motion. I can feel disaster slowly coming my way, and I can't stop it. I'm scared. What are my options? Waking up would be nice, but I can't do that either." He pounded is left hand repeatedly on the steering wheel. He tried to speak, stopped, took a breath and tried again. "I can't focus. I should have planned for this last fall, but I didn't think I would ever need to do it again. I was free and cured and happy and - " He smashed his left hand on the arm rest.

Breathing deeply he continued. "But I didn't plan ahead. I didn't think I would be here where I can't think. And now I don't know what to do. I thought I would be happy to get the grant to pursue my research, but then I thought, how does that get me closer to pastoral ministry? How does that accomplish our purpose in life, our commitment to each other? I've lost focus and don't know where to find it again. But, Beth, there is more. There is actually more that I haven't told you yet. Now it's my turn to say 'don't get upset'."

Beth looked at him with growing apprehension. What else could there possibly be?

Chapter 25
Further Explanations

"OK," the young man started slowly. "There is a reason I haven't told you this yet. It is because I simply don't understand it. I do understand my depression, but I don't understand the other things."

"What other things?" Beth replied. She tried to sound casual but her heart had begun to pound and a feeling of sick anxiety was gripping her insides.

"I'm sure you know what anxiety is," he continued.

If anyone knows what anxiety is, she thought, I am sure I know it right now. "Go on."

"It is different from my periods of depression. They come on and usually I can see them coming, not always, but often. They linger like a bad odor that can't be removed from your nose. You can blow your nose and try to smell something sweet, but the bad odor lingers. My periods of bad depression often linger for months, but sometimes less often. Unlike Daniel's first experience with the stampede, they don't last for a night. I know, Daniel didn't recover right away, but I made it seem to pass him quickly. Herds of buffalo were vast. Imagine you are in Nebraska; that really isn't too hard for us to imagine, but there is a herd of thirty million buffalo in North Dakota and they all want to go to Texas. They all have to go through Nebraska. They stampede; they stop to eat; they stampede again and then stop to eat again. It can take a long time for them all to get through Nebraska."

"I know your depression lasts. That isn't new. What is new? You asked if I knew what anxiety was and you are certainly making it build up."

"Yeah. Sorry. But we will get through this conversation and your anxiety will pass. We all have anxiety. We get anxious about a test, a big assignment, about a big change like marriage, about a variety of things. Right?"

Beth nodded and then gasped. "You're not getting anxious about our wedding and fearing it will prolong your depression are you?"

"No," the young man laughed. "I am not. I just used that as an unfortunate example. Anyway, we all get anxious from time to time; that is normal. Well, I often find myself getting anxious, really fearful, dreadfully fearful for no reason. Imagine you had a terrible nightmare. When you wake up you are anxious. After getting a drink and seeing reality, however, you can get over the anxiety. I can't."

"You have nightmares?"

"No, sweetheart, I don't have nightmares. I have daymares and much, much more. They come without warning. They debilitate me in profound ways. I feel frozen and can't act like I should in a given situation. They used to be just normal anxieties that I felt like everyone else, but in some ways they were deeper than others had. Now, they are coming at times that should not cause anxiety. The sky is blue, the birds are singing and everything is fine. I am not depressed. Then, Wham! Out of the blue someone says something and it triggers something in my mind and I gasp for breath. Nothing has changed around me. Only my pulse has become a jack hammer and I don't know what to do.

"There are some things that I do know that trigger it. When I think of being separated from you, it starts. I feel like a two year old who can't go to the nursery because he can't be away from his mother. I want to scream and cry and throw a fit, but that would be unseemly. Holding on to a rational thought, thinking through what is happening is impossible. All that I feel is the pounding fear in my chest and my mind doesn't want to work. I think for just a second that I want to pray but I can't. I can't hold that thought."

Beth placed her hand gently on his arm. "Is it just being away from me? Soon we will be together and you won't be away from me. It will be alright."

The young man sighed a long and expressive sigh. "No, Beth, it's not just that. I can wake up in a panic. Did I do this, or this or this? I can't just assure myself that I did even when I know I did. Then the panic starts again. It can be things like going back to my car again and again to make sure I locked the door. You would think that one time would be enough, right? Well, it isn't. How many times might I feel in my pocket to make sure I didn't leave my keys in the locked car, which, of course, may or may not still be locked? I can obsess about this until I get to class or work. That drives other thoughts away. I yell at myself, 'Don't be stupid', but then I recheck everything again anyway.

"And the odd thing is that it is random. Those things don't always happen, except the separation part, which I guess I remember even from childhood having felt that way when I went from my grandparents back to my own home. Anyway, they are random. I may go for a period of time without any attacks and live normally. Then, wham. There they are again."

Beth started to speak but he cut her off. "There is more," Beth. "This is where it gets desperate. I'm a song leader. I love Christian music. Think of all the hymns or songs that we sing that say we shouldn't be anxious or have a care. Think of how many songs say that we can just leave them all with Jesus and all will be well. Well, Beth, if you can't even pray, then you can't leave them anywhere. And if you can get around to praying you are afraid that you left out some detail that is important and on and on it goes. I know what the Bible says about 'be anxious for nothing but in all things with prayer and supplication let your requests be made known to God'."

The young man's voice started to rise in a panic. "I know all that. But when one of these attacks hits it's like I am drowning and all I want to do is breathe. Every thought is caught up on catching a single breath so that I don't die. My mind is frozen, absolutely frozen. And the problem is that it can be one thing today and a different thing tomorrow that brings these attacks. It's not always the same things. What I can't do today, I may perform with great ease tomorrow. What I can do today, I may not be able to do tomorrow.

"Beth, I am handing you a raw deal. I haven't tried to withhold this from you. It is so hard to explain I just don't know how to even explain it to you. You have to know it, though. You also have to know that I love you with my whole heart and I want to be your husband and love you for the rest of my life."

Again she reached her hand across the console and gently laid it on his arm. "I'll gladly take the raw deal if you are thrown in with it."

"One more thing, Beth. These attacks aren't like the depression. They are not constant and they don't last for days or weeks or months. They are not generally protracted but sometimes I can be in a general state of anxiety for longer and then have more frequent bouts of attacks. While I often know their triggers, I can't avoid the gun going off just the same. They are really attacks and they are scary. I think they are rather like the hawk and the rabbit. I know that Philip had depression, but I think he had panic attacks with them and that's what did him in. A panic attack or an attack of anxiety in the middle of a buffalo stampede is an incredibly awful experience.

"Then Beth, there is the frustration. I just get so frustrated at people who question my Christianity, my faith, my hope in Christ because of these things. There is such a stigma against any kind of mental illness in the church. Pastor Combes isn't alone and I fear I'll never get or keep a position just because of the prejudice. The next time Pastor runs extra long or starts in on the big five again, pull out your hymnal and look at all the hymns we have about joy and peace. They are beautiful and comforting and I love them, but they don't leave any room for the reality of depression or these attacks that I have.

"In my times of deepest depression I am still thankful for my salvation. When I think about popping myself off I am still glad that Jesus died to save me. When the depression is darkest I know that He loves me. I feel like Jeremiah in the middle of the book of Lamentations. He is bemoaning everything in his life and circumstances and then he says, 'God's compassions fail not. They are new every morning. Great is Thy faithfulness.' In the middle of massive depression he still knew God was there. Job did the same thing. When he was wishing he could die he still said, 'I know that in my flesh I will see God'. He had no idea that his depression would ever end. But he still believed in God.

"Beth, I still believe in God. My mind might be frozen and I might not be able to make a sound decision or even think about the future in a rational way, but my hope is still fixed on the truth of God's word and the assurance of His faithfulness. I wouldn't wish my pain on anybody, but I sure wish that others wouldn't say and do things to just make it worse."

Silently she prayed for him. He saw the tears begin to trail down her cheeks and was glad she could cry for both of them. "I have an idea," she finally said. "You can write. You can go to the safe room in your mind and write. You can use Daniel. He will help clear your thoughts. You can use his thoughts. Please write this weekend. Please, not for me, but for yourself. It will give you focus."

He nodded, quietly, lip quivering. "Thank you. Really, thank you. I love you. I will write this weekend. I will try to gain some focus from Daniel. But I am going to concentrate on just the one thing we were talking about before I dumped this new problem on you. First I must let Daniel help me get focused on the future.

Chapter 26
Plans for the Future

It was Christmas. Herr Schmitt had gathered all the community at the entrance to the cow barn. Since the November blizzard the roof supports had been reinforced and then reinforced again. Now they looked as if they might truly survive the winter. A surprisingly warm December sun bathed the back of the worshippers and the light winter wind that sang softly from the north was deflected away by the animal enclosure. The dairy cows had all come to the grating at the front of their pen as if they too wished to hear the Christmas message from Herr Schmitt. As the congregation sang their carols some cows mooed their own chorus.

With the last amen pronounced and buoyed by the cheerfulness of the weather, families dallied in the near knee deep snow to visit and share Yuletide greetings. Gradually they dispersed each to their own family celebration. Daniel and Tom had been asked to join the Schmitt's for theirs. Being the only two without a true family unit they were happy to accept the invitation. Frau Schmitt and Katrina fussed in the small space used as a kitchen. A traditional German Christmas dinner with all its fixings would have to wait until crops and trees were planted and yielded their abundance; until connections with the productivity of the civilized east could be more steady and secure; until more space could be created in the small house to make and store all that was necessary. For today they had made loaves of bread piled with an abundance of rich butter. The last remaining barrel of beer had been tapped but all knew it must be consumed slowly. An ample supply of smoked buffalo meat with a supporting cast of potatoes that were quickly aging without an adequate root cellar made a genuine feast.

For Daniel the meal was secondary to the time spent with Katrina. For everyone it was secondary to the joy of the day, the health of all in the community and the relaxation with good friends that the day afforded. After the meal was cleaned away they all sat together in the pleasant heat of the little stove. The bright sunlight streamed through the single glass paned window in the south wall. Its flood of watery light cheering those who realized that winter had, in fact, only begun.

The settlers had discovered that the vagary of Nebraska weather was more variable than the varied desires of seven expectant mothers. One day this and one day that. The snow from the Thanksgiving blizzard had largely melted under warm sunshine before being added to by other days of light snow. That in turn had melted and frozen again until there were layers of snow and ice throughout Martinsville. Today's welcome sun would simply mean that there would be another layer of ice by tomorrow. Still, it wasn't tomorrow; it was today and they sat and talked and rejoiced in the sunlight they had.

As topic drifted to topic Daniel excused himself and said he must run back to his own cabin for a moment. He quickly returned carrying his canvas bag. From it he produced four clumsily wrapped packages. The first he handed to Tom who slowly peeled off the old newspaper in which it was wrapped and held up his treasure for all to see. With tears stinging his eyes he thanked Daniel.

"I made it so you could always have your most important tools with you when you're working. I know you have five that you always seem to need. There is a pouch that will fit each of them and the strips of leather can tie around your waist so you will always have then handy."

Daniel presented a similar tool belt to Herr Schmitt and a comb for her bun that he had carved from a piece of buffalo rib was given to Frau Schmitt. He then asked Katrina to give him the present he had for Philip. She produced a far more neatly wrapped present and gave it to Daniel to give to her brother. In it was his knife, the one he had given Katrina after the Thanksgiving incident. During one of their weekly catechism sessions he had secured permission from Herr Schmitt that Philip could have it.

The fifth present he held in his trembling hand and then gave it to Katrina. She carefully unwrapped it as if were a noble gift from the Prince of Hess. Inside was a beautifully carved heart shaped pendant made from a piece of buffalo bone. On the back he had carefully burned the initials KS. A braided leather string made up the necklace that would hold it around her neck. The pendant was passed from hand to hand and Daniel was congratulated by everyone for his workmanship. Forgetting the propriety of the setting Katrina knelt to where Daniel was sitting and kissed him softly on his cheek.

Composing herself once again Katrina then handed Daniel a small rectangular present. He marveled at the sacrifice she had made to bring such fine paper all the way to Nebraska and then destroy it by using it to cover his gift. Fearful of doing further damage to the costly paper he unwrapped it with greatest care. Inside was a book. It was worn at the edges and written in a language he could not understand.

"That, Daniel," she beamed, "was my first primer in school. It is in German. Now that you speak it like a German you should learn to read it like a German." He looked inside the front cover. In a graceful hand was written on the top, "Daniel, Ich liebe dich, Katrina. Weihnachten 1855". She saw the puzzlement on his face at the inscription. "It says, Daniel, I love you, Katrina, Christmas 1855." He held it to his heart and slow tears danced from the corners of his eyes and down his cheeks.

Herr Schmitt cleared his throat. "Daniel, I too have a present for you." He gave Daniel another small rectangular present that was wrapped much as Daniel had wrapped his own. Daniel opened it slowly, but with less care. Inside was another book also written in what he could only assume was German. "Daniel, you have been an excellent student. You have memorized perfectly the

Ten Commandments, the Creed and the Lord's Prayer with all their questions. This was my catechism book when I was a boy. It will help you learn to read German because you already know what it says. We can also finish your catechism from it now as you learn German."

Daniel wiped his sleeve across his face. "Thank you. They are wonderful gifts."

Conversation drifted to plans for spring plantings and new work to be done in the community. Daniel was engrossed in watching Katrina and had only been half listening until the talk turned to plans for the settlement. He listened more carefully then until he was sure the conversation was about to turn again to a different topic.

"Herr Schmitt," he began, and once he had the attention of the adult men he continued. "There are a lot of children in Martinsville. I think they need a school. The building could be used for a school as well as a church. It could be used for town meetings. It doesn't have to be a fancy building, but it will need a stove and windows." He saw the interest and developing agreement in Herr Schmitt's eyes. Daniel swallowed hard. His heart was pounding as heavily as the ground shook when the buffalo stampeded. That brief thought gave him a start, but seeing Herr Schmitt eyeing him to know if Daniel had further comments, he forced himself to continue. "Herr Schmitt, I would like to be the teacher for the school."

Daniel tried to control his breathing but with little success. His heart continued its drumming against his chest. He remembered glumly the first time he had tried to speak up at the town meeting on the day they had arrived. The old fears clawed at his mind and the old urges to turn and run before destruction hit added restlessness to his feet. Even though the afternoon sun was fading and the house was getting cooler, he was getting warmer. Slowly he felt the choke hold lay against his throat and struggled just to get air. Tom watched him carefully knowing the sign of Daniel's increased anxiety. Katrina held her breath and waited with creeping fear as she saw Daniel's face turn red then pale. She saw his hands begin to tremble and wanted to rush to his side, save him, but her mother laid her hand on her shoulder and held her still.

Only seconds had passed but the hours contained in them continued to exert their strain on Daniel's mind. Herr Schmitt eyed him, waiting Daniel thought, to devour him. Panic pulsed harder in Daniel's veins. His eyes began to mist over and the room became vague. Still he did not run or fall on Tom's shoulder or bury his face into the hard floor and scream out his pain. Herr Schmitt drummed his fingers on his knees and watched Daniel struggle against himself. The passage of time, far less than the eons Daniel had experienced, had been merely thirty seconds. Then Herr Schmitt spoke.

"You are right, Daniel, we need a building for a church. I was just getting to that with Herr Miller. You have a good mind to add your thoughts at the right time. It would also be good to use it as a school. Right now all the mothers have their children to teach while there is so much more work to be done in feeding ourselves and preparing to survive another winter. As quickly as you have learned the catechism and also done your work and still made these beautiful gifts, I believe you can do many things well. I will discuss it with the other men. Now we must do our evening chores before dark."

All the men had gathered at the barns. Christmas or no Christmas each small shelter needed to be mucked every day. The pile of fertilizer for spring planting had grown into two piles and now three. Proportionately the mounds of hay were diminishing. While others mucked Herr Schmitt led Daniel to the two remaining cows still giving milk.

As they squeezed the rich creamy froth into buckets Herr Schmitt asked, "Daniel, you did not make all those fine presents just since Thanksgiving, did you?"

"No, sir, I started on them in early fall."

"So, when you had that incident at Thanksgiving, and I am sorry to discuss it, but when it happened you were working on gifts for us?"

"Yes, sir. I think now how strange it must seem. I was so looking forward to giving them, except the knife, to everyone. I didn't even think about that when, well, you remember."

"And how about the plans for a school and you being a teacher? How long have you had those?"

"After what happened Tom told me it might help if I made some real goals for the future. I couldn't tell him I had the goal of finishing all the presents, but I did tell him it was good idea. He also said if I saw myself as a more necessary part of things, a person with responsibilities that everyone would always count on, then maybe I could avoid another incident. I thought that was a good idea, too. I don't think, sir, that anything will ever stop the stampedes, but maybe if I keep real goals in front of me, goals that I must do each day to reach the next one, then I can keep from another incident. I hope that is true. Certainly my hope and joy and goal of marrying Katrina didn't stop me, but it just seemed so far away. I need to plan and work with goals to reach more goals. Herr Schmitt, I love your daughter so much. I never want to hurt her. I will try whatever ideas I can to help me do that."

"So, Daniel, is teaching school just a goal, or is it something you really want to do?"

"Will you promise not to laugh if I tell you what I really want to do? Will you?"

"If it is good for my Katrina, I promise."

"Herr Schmitt, I want to be a pastor. I want to tell others about the goodness and grace of God. I want them all to have the joy I had when you told me. I have never lost that joy, Herr Schmitt. Even that day when you saved my life, even in the midst of a buffalo stampede, I have always believed what you said and it brings me joy. Why would I do something like I did; I don't know. The devil just ambushed me. I haven't said anything about what I really want to do because if the devil can ambush me I may not be good enough to be a pastor. But that's what I want to be."

Herr Schmitt wiped the streaming tears from his face. Coughing roughly to regain control of his voice he replied. "Daniel, the Bible says that if a fellow Christian is overtaken in sin, then others are supposed to help him. You will be a wonderful helper, Daniel, to many people. You know what it means to be ambushed by the devil. It may not be the last time Daniel that it will happen, but the righteous man falls seven times and rises again. Being a teacher will be good practice for you. God is going to greatly bless you and Katrina."

Chapter 27
Driving Home

"Look in the notebook on top of everything in the back seat, Beth" the young man coming of age said. "I hope it helps."

As he drove she read and then reread the chapter. "How is this going to help?"

"Daniel was still in a buffalo stampede when Tom told him to make goals that were reachable in order to reach goals farther ahead. I have always tended to look far out. I take too little thought about tomorrow in relation to how it fits into the next year or five years. I see where I want to go in five years or for a life, but I have never thought about it taking tomorrow to get there. It is either a character flaw or part of all the wrong things in my brain. I am the world's worst day to day planner. I know you are different. Maybe you are even normal, no, I mean the norm. My brain usually feels like a pinball machine. It's popping all over everywhere in random zigs and zags with just the goal of not losing the game."

"So now you are going to plan better?"

"So now you are going to help me plan better. Daniel is safe. He gets things right on his own. He's the real deal, and there are many people just like him. I wish I were. The only time I can hold a thought is when I am writing. Otherwise it is just ping, ping, ping, ping like the ball in the machine."

"So what do you want to do tomorrow? I'll write it down."

"Marry you. I have no other plans or goals. I just want to marry you."

"And that didn't help Daniel, did it. He wanted to marry Katrina but it was too far away for him to focus. I want you to be alive to marry me. Do you understand?"

"OK. Tomorrow I have to go to school and go to work. I don't want to do either. Tomorrow I want to marry you." He saw her sharp eyes flash an instant warning to stop. "So what else should I want to do tomorrow? What can you think of that I should do tomorrow to help with some long term goal? This is another area of anxiety, but different. I get stuck, things get out of order and I can't rearrange them. Then I panic and just stand still in fear. If someone doesn't come along and say, 'Let's do this first and then you can do this and this', you know, order my life, then I either stop or abandon doing that thing and leave it. Notice I said the person says, 'let us', well that is key. Someone helps me get back into order and then with step by step directions I can take off again. I am really glad you haven't run away yet in fear.

"Imagine, Beth, looking at a giant room that is a mess and you know it has to be cleaned. That is often my mind or my plans. They have fallen into total disarray. Then imagine that you look at the mess and say there is no way I know how to even start cleaning this up and getting these things organized. The mess just grows and you hate it so you avoid that room. But then someone comes and says, 'Let's pick up all the books first. We will throw all the other things off the book shelf and put the books on it.' So you do. Then they say, 'Now, let's pick up all the toys and put them in this box.' So you do. Then they say, 'Now you can pick up so and so and put it there and such and such and put it there and this and that and put it here.' Now I do it and am happily along my way. I just couldn't get over the panic, or anxiety, of the mess to get started. Oddly, my love, I don't freeze up when helping someone else. I can clearly help them see and offer the kind of guidance I need. It is the strange case of the physician who can't heal himself.

"But, we were talking about our future on the way home. It's a mess and I need help to get things started. Beth, can you save me? Will you save me and keep me? I really can lead if I can get the messes sorted out. If they accumulate again, you can organize my thoughts and I can lead again. Will you, Beth, will you help me so that I can lead?"

She rested the tip of her pen on her lips and stared straight ahead. Her mind didn't work like his, of that she was sure. She never remembered her thoughts ever pinging around in her mind like a pinball. She couldn't imagine what it would be like to have that every day. How could she help organize a mind that was always on the move? How could she help organize a mind that was stuck in fear? She certainly believed he thought that way. Somehow he had managed to control it well enough to be an honor student. That was an absolute incongruity to her.

Can I really do this all my life? The sudden thought chilled her. She was committed to him. She loved him. But she was now confronted with something more concrete than a disease of the mind. His mind had a symptom, no, multiple symptoms and she was now called upon to offer a cure. Could she really offer a cure, or was it just a crutch, for the rest of her life. Day after day after day for years and years, could she help him focus on what was needed today to get to someday? She sighed and looked at him. Of course she could; she loved him. Well, if I'm going to do it, I had better start. O, ideas, ideas, I need just one of you, give me one idea.

"Where are we going on our honeymoon?" she asked.

"I thought we agreed on St. Louis, didn't we?"

"We did. Have you chosen any hotels or motels? Will we drive straight to St. Louis after the wedding? That's a long trip. Have you thought of a place to stop for the night? You do want to stop for the night, don't you?" she added with a coy smile.

"That was four questions, to which I answer three no's and a yes to the last one."

"Then for tomorrow we will put down, take your atlas from your car into your apartment and plan a route. For the next day we will put visit a few motels in town and get a list of their motels on the way to St. Louis and in St. Louis. No, let's make that go to one motel each day for the rest of the week. That will give you a whole week of things to do each day."

"Sounds like something I can do. We won't worry about the following week until next weekend. Is that OK?" Assuming it was, he went on. "Tell me about your weekend."

Beth related a variety of events, each minor but all meaningful. "But there was one big problem," she added. "I had a book that I got in 9th grade. It is really, really important to me that I find that book. I looked for it over Christmas break and Mom has been looking for it for the past three weeks. We can't find it anywhere. It is so frustrating."

"What is it?"

"I'm not going to tell you right now. It is very important to me to find it. It has answers to something that I can't quite remember. It's interesting. You'll enjoy it. No, you'll love it. I want to take it with us on our honeymoon and when we can't find anything else more interesting to do; I want to read it to you. You can lie in the sun by the pool and I will read. We can take walks like you always want to do, and when we sit in the shade of a big old tree, I will read it to you. As we drive all those miles in the car I will read it to you. I really mean it; you will love it. But I can't find it and I am not going to tell you what it is until we go on our honeymoon."

They drove along in amicable silence. She was absorbed in what she hoped to find in her book. It was going to make a big difference to both of them; she was sure. She just couldn't remember the particulars and the harder she thought the more elusive they became. Gradually she dozed off.

The young man, left happily to his own thoughts, let them drift back to his dear friend Daniel. He was at least going to get married sooner than the young man. He was happy for him and wondered what a new spring and a new life together would bring him.

Chapter 28
Spring

Spring had broken gloriously over the wide and fertile expanse of Nebraska prairie. Earth sighed out its frost and inhaled the luxurious warmth of longer days. Birds again danced along a trail of tall grass stems and bees again pollinated colorful flowers. Life, beautiful and abundant, rose from the long cold death of winter.

The citizens of Martinsville had rejoiced in the resurrection of their Savior at an open-air sunrise service. With the coming of April they had forced their steel plows into the hard sod of the virgin prairie. A few weeks later they had celebrated the nuptials of Daniel Cooper and Katrina Schmitt. The following day Tom Miller surrendered his cabin as the new nest for the young couple. He led a small convoy of wagons; each pulled by eight horses and filled with buffalo hides headed east to Council Bluffs to trade for needed supplies. They would need things both for the settlement and to sell to wagon trains that passed their way the coming summer.

Between the breaking of the sod and the tying of the knot the community had come together for an important meeting. Herr Schmitt laid out the need for a building that could serve as both school and church. Unanimous accord was reached on the proposed project with little necessary discussion. But then Herr

Schmitt introduced the second part of the plan. Daniel would be presented as the candidate to teach the school.

Albert Gelt stood at once to question the choice of Daniel. "Certainly, we all respect the work that Daniel does in and for our community. No word of reproach can be brought against his life of integrity. However, Herr Schmitt, he is but a new convert to our faith. Do you really propose that one so new could properly teach our children? Also is he equipped with enough knowledge of German and the subjects he will teach to undertake such a great responsibility over our children? "

"Dearest friend," Herr Schmitt replied, "would you like to question Daniel as to the particulars of the catechism or the confession? Would you like to question his knowledge of any subject he may be called upon to teach? If so, please do so now in the presence of all."

"Thank you, Herr Schmitt. I would indeed question him before all."

"Before you do, Herr Gelt, please everyone know that they may join in the questioning."

A murmur of assent passed through the gathered assembly. For nearly an hour they asked, and with great poise, Daniel confirmed his knowledge of subjects and understanding of the faith. When no further questions were offered Herr Gelt said, "I raise no further objections."

Before Herr Schmitt could rise to confirm Daniel's appointment another voice broke the peace of the meeting. "Herr Schmitt and gathered friends, there is more to be concerned about than Daniel's fitness with the catechism. There is the genuine concern of his mental and emotional ability to fill such an important role. Is it not true, Herr Schmitt, that Daniel is plagued by emotional instability? Have you not had to raise your own hand to protect him from deadly self harm? Can we trust such a person to be safe with our children?"

Herr Schmitt, with controlled fire in his eyes, turned to the new speaker. "Herr Dietrich, have you so long worshipped beside Daniel, taken the body and blood of our Savior at his side, shared the common confession and received the common absolution with him and still regard him as a danger to your children? Have you offered him the blessings of the Lord with hypocrisy? Have you ever questioned him privately about these things? Then why do it now?"

"I can, Herr Schmitt," Peter Dietrich responded testily, "forgive him his sins without being concerned about his stability. I can care for him without hypocrisy without entrusting my children into the care of someone who may lose self control and kill himself in front of them!" A slight sprinkling of approval to the new objection and explanation passed through the group.

Daniel had faced the questions of his competency with great trembling of heart but without fear of error. Now the blood pulsed through his veins like the Platte in flood. It raged and his head felt the throb of pain as his heart felt the sharp stab of rejection. Was it always to be his fate to see and hear the Reverend Stout call out his failings? His eyes began to lose their focus on the crowd of friends he had come to love and trust. His hands shook and his legs trembled as he fought for control. Was he really unfit? What if the buffalo began to stampede in the middle of a school day? What if one of Philip's hawks caught a rabbit outside the school window? Would he fail to keep his composure or would the screams do to him what they had to Philip?

For the past three weeks Daniel had seen the bull buffalo pawing the earth and walking slowly toward him. The bright sounds of the prairie that brought great joy had also turned to the quick sounds of death and sadness. For nearly a month increased anxiety about the changes that would come with his marriage had fought to overcome the joyous anticipation of the event. Through it all he had pursued his studies with Herr Schmitt and Katrina in both doctrine and German. The struggle to do either had clashed with the known reward of doing both. More than once he knew, like no one else, that he had cast his eyes too long on the knife in the barn. Daniel felt the comforting hand of Frau Schmitt on his arm and Tom's hand on his shoulder. But over the head of them both he could see his pa and Reverend Stout, each smirking, "You can't escape him, Daniel, the devil has you by the nose and by the toes."

Daniel wondered if he should stand and try to speak, but he knew if he stood he would either faint or run. That would decide the question now before the assembly. The roar of Reverend Stout's voice echoed from each corner of his mind. He stifled a screaming response as he tried to focus on what was now being said, but it was just a blur behind the raging tornado of old accusations. Could he ever do what he wanted? Could he ever reach a goal? Would Katrina be better off without him? The cyclone in his mind kept spinning the questions faster and faster until he felt himself being jerked to his feet.

Herr Schmitt's voice broke harshly through the storm. "Now, Daniel, now you must respond. No one can do it for you."

Daniel gazed around at the assembled members of his community. Yes, he said to himself, it is really my community. From face to face he turned his gaze. Some bowed their heads to avoid making contact with his sad eyes. Others appeared as distortions of people, exaggerated in various ways, some with large heads and bulging eyes that stared into his soul, some with inflated lips that laughed scornfully at him and still others with overgrown hands that put real buttons on overgrown lips mocking his silence. Then beside him he sensed another and it was Katrina. Not again, his mind screamed, not again shall she have to speak for me.

Slowly and softly he began. "I cannot deny any accusations brought against me by Herr Dietrich." Herr Dietrich rose to deny that he had made any accusations but Daniel, to his own surprise, raised his hand and said with stiff conviction, "Oh, yes, they were accusations. They were the common accusations that a person who suffers from melancholy is unfit for any task of responsibility in Christ's Church. I have heard them, and they were once true.

"They were true before Herr Schmitt showed me the way to Christ. In Christ I am fit for the tasks He calls me to do. I can never promise that I will not be sad in front of your children. I can never promise that I will not be overcome by tears when a strong wave of depression rolls over me. I can never promise that I will always be eager and strong to do the job of teaching that I long to do and not be undermined by insipient and unexplained sorrows. But I promise you that by God's grace and your effectual prayers that I will fulfill the responsibilities placed upon me to the glory of God the Father Almighty." With that he sat down, surprised and exhausted.

Herr Schmitt rose and addressed the community. With tears in his eyes he spoke in a broken voice. "Friends, for many years I have held a story in my heart; a tragic story that burdens me whenever I think of it. I have only told it twice in the many years since it happened. One day Frau Schmitt found me crying in the barn. It was the anniversary of the event. Last summer I shared the story with Katrina and Daniel. Now I shall share it with you." Carefully he retold his tale, sometimes with strength but often through tears.

"Now, my friends, I know much about such tragedy of mind and life. Yes, I have had to intervene with Daniel to prevent the sad story from going on. Still, I have given him permission to marry my Katrina and I expect him, through all the struggles of his mind and emotions, to care for her as God has directed. Philip felt alone. We do not want Daniel to feel the same way. He already feels so alone in his mind and heart that he should not have to experience the same from those who could truly love him. Again, I present Daniel as the candidate to teach our children."

Silence settled over the assembly. Some shook their heads. A few of those in concern at the decision they would have to make; the others because they had already made theirs. Others in the congregation bowed their heads and prayed for guidance and for Daniel. After several minutes of silence Albert Gelt rose and declared, "I support this decision. How many will join me in doing so?"

Of the sixteen men in the room eleven hands were raised. "How many of you will then help to build our needed building including a small addition for Daniel and Katrina to live in?" Slowly all sixteen men raised their hands. The work would begin when the crops were in. Daniel received the congratulations of those who had supported him and the promise of help from them all. But as the assembly broke up the buffalo began to stampede, were unabridged even by the joy of nuptials and pounded across the vast prairie of his emotions and mind into the summer.

Chapter 29
Katrina's Journal

The "I do's" had been spoken. The song the young man had written for his bride had been beautifully sung. Her parent's neighbor had been momentarily embarrassed at the reception when she had mistaken the young man for one of Beth's old boyfriends. The cake had been eaten the good-byes said. Then they had gone to Beth's house and changed their clothes and left on the honeymoon that Beth had carefully scheduled items for the young man to complete and have it all prepared.

"You really don't mind the plans we have made after our honeymoon, do you?" he asked.

"Dahhrrrrling," she teased, "nothing could make me happier than to live in a tent for three months." Before he could misinterpret her words she quickly added, "It will be great training for being missionaries. If we can live in a tent in the woods for three months, we can live anywhere. It is a good step in long term preparation for our goals."

"I'm glad you take such a positive approach, Dahhrrlling," he jested back. "I also think that working with the children will be good preparation. If I like it as much as I think I will then I will get a provisional certificate to teach this fall. If I still like it we can return to university and I can get my degree in education as well. It should take only a year. Perhaps teaching in a mission school would be further progress to becoming church planting missionaries. I commend you, my dearest wife, for your skillful scheduling to help me reach longer term goals. Sadly for you, you are now stuck with both me and that job forever."

"And it shall be my highest goal in life to do them both well, Dahhrrrlinng."

He saw the glint of happiness in her eyes and was assured of her sincerity. Why, he asked himself, did Daniel have to send his stupid herd of buffalos chasing down my neck as well as his. I should be on top of the world right now, but I fear every word she says may be poking fun at what we will be doing. How many new brides in their right minds would be content to leave the comforts of hot water and electricity to live in a tent? None! That's right; so either she is as much out of her mind as I am, or I really did find one in a million. She seems sane enough, not that I am a good judge of sanity, but she really probably is. So, I got the one in a million.

"Penny for your thoughts," Beth intruded on his musings.

"I was just thinking how lucky I am to have married you. You are either as nuts as me or one in a million, and I will go with the latter. When I told everyone what we were doing this summer, no one believed you were really happy about it. I have greatly doubted it, too. But you really don't seem to be upset. You are truly a wonder woman to me."

"It really is going to be good training. You never know what kind of place we might have to live in on the mission field. Besides that we will get to work together, see each other all the time and the only place we can go from here is up. Running water would be up. Electricity would be up. Think about it, we are getting a chance to begin our life together on the ground floor and move up together. I think that is special."

Beth brought a book from her purse and continued, "Think of how little Daniel and Katrina had. They would be without running water or electricity or gas stoves or refrigerators for most of their lives; maybe all their lives. He loved her and she loved him. Don't you think that is all we will need? We have love and each other. God will take care of the rest."

"Well, my wonderful, beautiful and intelligent wife, you have done well in supporting me in the ways I told you might help."

"And my genius and handsome husband, I am glad to do so. It even seems to me that you are still under the buffalo stampede that began in March. Right?"

"I hate to admit it on our wedding day, but yes."

"Then let me begin to read you the book that Mom finally found buried in my hope chest. I think you will be surprised and happy and maybe cheered a little from your depression."

And so Beth began to read. "The Hill County Historical Society is happy to reproduce an abridged version of the diaries of Katrina Wilson (nee Ohrtmann), one of the original settlers of Martinsburg, the original white settlement of Hill County. Katrina and her family, along with eighteen other families settled the town of Martinsburg, Nebraska in June of 1855. She was the eldest child of Johann Ohrtmann and Maria Ohrtmann. They also had a son Philip who would become a prominent personality in Hill County history."

The young man slowed the car and pulled to the side of the road. Turning to Beth he tried to say something and failed. Pointing at the book he finally stuttered, "Is that for real?"

"Yes, dear husband of my heart, it is. It is the book I had been looking for. You will want to hear all of it, but it will take more time than we have on this trip to do it. Pay attention to the road and enjoy the rest of your story."

He pulled back on the road while she went on. "Right now I am just reading the introduction. I have to do so, so that you can keep all the players straight. I will go on.

"All the original settlers of Martinsburg were German immigrants with the exception of Asa Wilson and James George (JG) Madison. Asa was the ward of JG and the two had been picked up on the trail by the German wagon train. Madison's wife, Rose, had died early in the trek west and while the rest of their train continued, Madison and Asa had lingered at Rose's graveside for a week and eventually joined the German colony and became active members of it.

"Asa and Katrina would become central to the life of the settlement for the next sixty years. By that time Martinsburg was gradually receding from existence and today is marked only by the old church graveyard and a plaque on the church's original foundation. The journals contained in this book were donated by Marie Wilson Schmitt and Otto Wilson, the eldest children of Asa and Katrina Wilson. The Wilsons had nine children, six of which survived infancy. Johann Ohrtmann died in 1871 and Maria in 1878. Their graves are in the Hope of Christ Lutheran Church cemetery in Martinsburg.

JG Madison will be mentioned little in this abridged journal so a note should be made concerning him as well. In the summer of 1856, on the second wagon train to pass through the settlement of Martinsville, there was a young widow, Martha Owens, with two small children. Her husband had died in a wagon accident near the point where JG and Asa had buried Rose. Her husband was buried next to Rose's grave and the site became known as Madison Cemetery as many more emigrants who died early on the trail were buried there. Martha decided not to continue to Oregon but to stay a short time in Martinsburg until she could return home to Illinois. But instead of returning home she married JG Madison and together they had five children, four who survived infancy. Madison, who had planned to farm in Oregon, changed his plans from farming and ran a cartage business that proved instrumental to the success of the Martinsburg community.

"The families of JG Madison and Asa Wilson would intertwine over the years. Philip Ohrtmann would marry, Hazel, the eldest of Martha Madison's two daughters that arrived with her in Martinsburg. Asa and Katrina's second daughter, Elisabet, would marry JG and Martha's eldest son, John Madison. Asa and Katrina, James George and Martha, and Philip and Hazel are all buried in the Hope of Christ Lutheran Church cemetery."

Beth turned to the young man. "This is very interesting, don't you think?" He nodded and she continued. "There is another important part of the genealogy that is not included in this book.

Philip and Hazel had a daughter, Esther, who went off to the Nebraska Normal School to become a teacher. She had planned to return to Martinsburg to teach in the school there. But when she was at school she met a young German immigrant who was not Lutheran. He was Brethren, but she fell in love with him anyway much to her family's disapproval. Ironically, his name was Martin. They moved to Council Bluffs where Martin became a pastor. He and Esther had a son and named him Wilbur, Wilbur Beck was my grandfather. Wilbur married Lillian Conrad, who was Presbyterian and he converted to her church. Their daughter also went to teacher's college and married my father. You can see that the many changes in names might hide the fact that I am directly connected to your characters. Your characters are fiction, but they are very historically accurate fiction."

Again the young man pulled off the road. "Do you mean that you knew all of these things this whole time?"

"No, the names were different for most of the characters. I hadn't read it since I was in 9th grade and didn't even read it very carefully then. It is what is still to come, though, that I think will be so important and hopeful for you. But first, how did you pick your characters and why did you place them in Martinsville?"

"I hadn't planned on there even being a Martinsville. It wasn't until Sally died that I decided on putting Daniel and Tom in Nebraska. Many Germans really were early settlers there so it was a natural fit to call it Martinsville. Daniel needed support so I had to research someone to give him hope. I came up with Lutherans. They really did believe that way about depression. It all came together. The impossibility of the connections are beyond imagination, but I am interested in hearing more of her journal."

"Good. We have nothing else to do for five days," she laughed, "so we can make some real progress." Her husband groaned and she laughed harder.

Chapter 30
Progress

Working with the children at camp had been even more fulfilling than the young man coming of age had expected. In the fall he obtained his provisional teaching license and worked as a substitute teacher which he also enjoyed. With Beth making his schedules and him carefully following them he was again enrolled at university to earn a degree in education.

"Honey," Beth asked as they unpacked their things in their new apartment, "if you could come back here for a degree in education, why couldn't you have just gone straight to seminary? I waited to ask until we got here because I didn't want to pressure you. Now that we are here, however, I want to know without forcing you into any kind of change in our plans."

The young man sat down on the couch and pulled her onto his lap. "It goes back to not liking change. Getting married is a big change, but it is the best one I have ever made. Coming back here keeps everything else familiar. Our folks are just three hours away. My aunt and uncle live here in town and love us deeply. I already know this school and am comfortable here.

"Did you know that my parents lived in married student housing when they went here; right on this very spot where these new apartments are? Did you know that I lived here with them and some of my earliest memories come from being on this campus? Did you know that my aunt had a job ringing the chimes at the center of campus each day? I haven't been run over by a buffalo since last July. I want to keep it that way as long as possible. Familiar is good."

"But you are still going to have to work like you would have at seminary; work at a job I mean. Won't that bring on anxiety and stress and lead to another stampede?"

"If only it was anxiety and stress that brought on stampedes I would be happy. They come when the sun is shining and the birds are singing and boys and girls are getting married. As to a job, yes I will work, but I can get a job on campus and that will make it easier.

"At seminary I would have had to take out a loan. I don't want to go into debt. Then I would be stressed and anxious and then if the buffalo came I would be a wreck. This is a slow and safe transition in life."

"But I could work full time so you wouldn't have to take out too big a loan," Beth replied. "I want to stand beside you and help you."

"You have to manage my whole life, Beth. That is a huge job by itself. But there is a lot more to it than that. I've never told you much about my dad. It is a story that reminds me all the time of how I don't want to be.

"My mother always wanted to stay home and be a housewife and mother. That was her goal in life. My dad said she must work to pay the bills, and there were a lot of bills. If my dad had three cents he would convince a friend to give him two more. Now he had a nickel. He would leverage that nickel through pure schmooze into a dime. All our life we lived seven cents on the dollar in debt. He once got her a brand new car for her birthday and when she asked him how he could afford it he told her that he had signed a contract for her to teach at an area school the next year.

"Carolyn broke up with me because I was just like my dad. I emotionally cheated on her. I lied to her. I was living like I had seen life lived. I wasn't happy living that life as a child and I didn't think I could go on living that life as an adult. When I became a Christian I was able to leave that life mostly behind. We all sin, so I couldn't leave it all behind all the time, but I want to. I don't want to make you pay our bills. I will work forty hours a week and take a full load just like I did when we were going together. I am dependent on you to live. That is burden enough."

"You know, dear, that I really think you are crazy; crazy in love with me," she laughed.

In mid-semester the young man came running into their apartment. "Beth," he called, "I have just heard the greatest thing today in class." Beth came into the living room and waited for him to continue. "There is a new type of education that is being offered all over the country. It isn't totally new. But it is new as a means to earn an accredited degree and even graduate degrees. You know all those cheap ads you see that say, 'Learn how to be a detective at home'? Well, correspondence schools are starting to become legitimate options for graduate school.

"Think of it. What if I could find a seminary that was a correspondence school as well as a brick and mortar school? What if I could earn my degree on my schedule while doing my job as a teacher? What if it were affordable and there would be no debt at all? You wanted a job, my dearest truest love. Well I have one for you."

Beth flopped on the couch and pulled him down beside her. "You want me to do research? You know I hate doing research and that I am terrible at it."

"Yes, O love of my life, I know. But I don't think you would be able to find anything about seminaries offering correspondence classes for a degree in the college library. But you love going to the public library. They have Christian magazines there. Just sit and read through a few of them and see if they have ads for anything like that. Then you can put following up on those things on my schedule. How about that?"

"Well, dear, that is something that I can do. But I want to tell you that your schedule might be getting a lot busier very soon."

"We're going to have a baby!" he gasped. "Really?"

"No, not really. Pastor Allen called today and said he wants you to consider taking a part-time position at the church as youth leader. I will tell you his exact words. 'Your husband's faithfulness and knowledge have been noticed by members of the board. They want to expand our youth program and want to ask him to do it. I am just giving you a head's up about what you will hear tonight at church.' And that was the entire conversation. Your faithful study of the Bible has already moved you into a new ministry. Isn't that exciting?"

He pulled her close and kissed her warmly. "That is wonderful news. Finding a new church when we moved back here was a real blessing. But, what if they find out about me? Then what?"

"If they want you now, why wouldn't they want you then? Did you think of that?"

"What about Pastor Combes He wouldn't have wanted me if he knew and he had handpicked me as his minister of music. Loving me upfront and loving me when they know the truth are two different things."

"Are you always going to hesitate to take a position because of what they might do later? You will never get a position if you do."

"No, O dearest of the dear, I will take it. It just gives me a stab of anxiety to think about down the road to when love turns to hate. I hurt in advance."

"Take no thought of tomorrow, dear, for today has enough worry of its own. Somebody even wiser than you said that."

He kissed her again. "I would die without you; you know that don't you?"

"I know," she laughed while flipping her long brown hair across his face, "that I am truly indispensible. That is why you are going to take me out to supper tonight and bribe me to start on your research tomorrow."

"Does Micky Dee's still have a burger, fries and a drink with change back from a buck?" She nodded with a big smile. "Well, O love of my life, I have two dollars in my pocket so I offer you up to half of my kingdom."

Beth began her search for seminaries offering correspondence programs the next day. The first three magazines she read had nothing to offer so she decided to go to the church and look through their library. Pastor Allen was just bringing in the mail when she arrived.

"Looking for a correspondence seminary? Is that right? Well, we get this newspaper from a mission agency each month and it has a section at the back on schools. You can check there. It just came today and I don't usually read it. Take it and I hope it helps. It will be good for him to get more education and these correspondence seminaries are starting to expand and new ones are popping up to offer just what he is looking for."

Beth took her treasure home and left the back page with all the correspondence schools open and lying on her husband's desk. While sitting at his desk, feeling his presence and wishing so much that he didn't have to work all the time and go to school she was struck with an idea. She pulled out his typewriter and rummaged through the desk drawers until she found the manuscript for Buffalo Stampede. Sliding a sheet of paper into the machine she began to pound away. She had just finished two chapters of typing and put everything back where she found it when he came home.

"Dahhrlling," she purred, "I have been a dutiful little wife today and done as you asked." She kissed his cheek and pointed her finger to the newspaper on top of the desk. "You see, O great lord of my realm, your every wish is my command." Then kissing him on the nose she bounced into the kitchen and prepared supper.

Each day thereafter she worked on his manuscript until she came to the last chapter. It wasn't done. He hadn't finished it. She sat and pouted. He worked so hard and studied so hard and now he had the extra job at the church. She couldn't ask him to work on his book as well. But thinking of Katrina's journal, she knew that she could finish the last chapter for him.

Chapter 31
Katrina

"Papa," Katrina cried, "why can't I make Daniel happy? I think that he is suffering from a buffalo stampede, but he hasn't told me. It just seems that way. Shouldn't being married make him happy? O, Papa, can you talk to him?"

"My precious jewel, I cannot talk to him. I love you and want the best for you, and that best is that I not interfere in your marriage." Herr Schmitt went to his book shelf where he still had the treasured library given to his father. "Here, my little dove, is advice from Dr. Luther. You can encourage him with Scripture. Just don't go pointing your finger in his chest and saying, 'now hear the word of the Lord'." Katrina stopped sniffling and laughed at the picture of her doing that to Daniel. "Daniel is quick to memorize things. Suggest that you memorize together the twenty-third psalm. Then think of other passages in the Bible that speak of our tender Shepherd and memorize them together as well. It will bless you both.

"Now here is another suggestion by Dr. Luther. As much as is possible never let him be alone. He works with the other men all day, but when he is home, you must always be there, too. Dr. Luther also says that a full belly can make a man feel better. Make sure he eats even if he says he isn't interested. Finally, little one, Dr. Luther tells the young men, if they have a girl, to think about her." Herr Schmitt tenderly kissed Katrina's forehead and smiled. "Give him something to think about."

Katrina blushed, kissed her papa and ran back to her chores. These are all things I can do, she thought. I cannot drive away the buffalo, but I can make him feel a little less pain. With each potato she planted in the huge community garden she thought of different ways to lift Daniel's spirit. He loves music, she mused. Maybe he knows some hymns from his childhood that he remembers with fondness. He could teach me and we could sing them together. Maybe we need to walk out on the prairie more in the evening. On and on her mind drifted as she stooped over the freshly broken earth to provide meals for their winter feasting.

Daniel sank his spade deep into the bare earth. A small section of land had been cleared of the hard prairie sod and designated for the church and school building with an addition for Daniel and Katrina. Daniel and several other men were digging a trench for the foundation. Each day after the noon meal they devoted two hours to this project while other men dug a foundation for the new dairy barn. A late April snow had slowed their progress and they hoped it hadn't been disastrous for Tom and those with him on their way to Council Bluffs.

Those working with Daniel chatted with each other while they dug. Daniel didn't feel like talking. He saw how much work remained and felt it would never be finished. The others congratulated themselves on how much progress they had made. Daniel discovered he had just been leaning on his spade instead of digging with it when Herr Gelt slapped him on the back and laughingly said, "Dreaming about Katrina, are you? We'll get this built and then you will have a fine bed to dream in." The others all laughed. Their good natured laughter suddenly made Daniel feel like laughing too and he dug away with earnest until their shift was done.

Spring turned to summer and summer to late summer, a season all its own on the prairie. Eight wagon trains had stopped in their settlement for rest and supplies. Tom had made a second trip to Council Bluffs and was now away on his third. Sometimes men from the wagons would pitch in and help with the building of the church and barn in exchange for goods they could not afford to buy. Progress had speeded up with their assistance and the inaugural service of the new building was planned for the first Sunday in September. They had three weeks and a lot of finishing work to go.

Old Sol was in a terrible mood that day, angry at the earth and the men on it. He blazed his wrath across the increasingly dry earth that lay victim to his angry frown. Men sat more than they worked. Women soothed the crankiness of tired and hot children. The cows were balky and the horses reticent to take a harness. Martinsville knew they could expect no more help from passing trains this season. What was left was left for them alone and each breath of scorched air sapped more of their strength to do it.

Across a rise just south of the settlement they saw a lone rider approaching. A lone stranger on such a hot day was unusual. The citizens of Martinsville lingered in what shade they could find and watched him approach. Waves of heat rising from the searing earth sometimes made it seem as if more than one rider was coming, but gradually only the one came to a stop at the horse trough.

"Greetings," he called to them in German. At the sound of their language several men heaved themselves from their shady retreats and went to meet the stranger. He slid from his saddle and shook the hand of each man who approached. "My name is Otto Krueger." He had a warm smile to accompany his clear and pleasant voice. "I am assigned by the Missouri Lutheran district president to meet the people in the settlements of North Kansas and up to the Platte. I am to see if there are spiritual needs for leadership among the German settlements and offer assistance as much as I am able."

Herr Schmitt welcomed him and made introductions. Then with a great sense of civic pride he showed him the new church and school that was being built. "Are you, Herr Schmitt, serving here as spiritual leader?" Pastor Krueger asked. "How can I help?"

"It is our goal, Pastor, to finish this building and have our dedication service on the first Sunday of September. Are you free to stay that long and minister the sacrament and dedicate the building with us? A week after we dedicate the building we will be starting a school in it as well. Let me introduce you to the young man who will be the teacher." Herr Schmitt saw Daniel approaching to join the group. "Here he is, Pastor Krueger. Daniel is a fine young man who has shown great skill in Lutheran doctrine and good aptitude in the knowledge needed to teach our children. And," he winked, "he is married to my daughter, so I know that he is a very smart man with discriminating tastes. But come, let us get out of this infernal sun and get you refreshment."

Everyone was happy to have a legitimate excuse for taking the rest of the afternoon off. The whole community gathered in the unfinished barn, which was airier than the church, and got acquainted with the visitor. Daniel realized that as the school teacher and a recognized person of importance in the community he should be more engaged with the visitor, but he held back. Would the arrival of this stranger change his hopes and dreams of becoming a pastor? Would, indeed, a new pastor also insist on teaching the school as well? Daniel was wracked with spasms of anxiety.

Katrina slid up beside him and held his hand. "A penny for your thoughts, dear?"

"They aren't worth a penny," he sighed. "They are wrong and corrupt. They come from my failed and broken mind."

"Then let us go and get some encouragement from Pastor Krueger. Papa has been boasting about you for the past hour and Pastor Krueger wants to meet the man who will teach our school and someday become a great preacher. That is what Papa called you – the man who will become a great preacher. Everyone has told him that the great preacher can be a little shy at the start but now they are all waiting for you."

Herr Schmitt had much he wanted to share in private with Pastor Krueger and so he was invited to spend his time in the settlement living in their house. "Pastor Krueger," he began when they were alone after supper, "I must speak to you privately about Daniel. He is a wonderful boy. But he has some problems that need to be discussed. They are not terrible sins or matters of behavior.

"Daniel suffers greatly from melancholy. He demonstrates great faith and obedience to the Word, but it does not keep him from deep bouts of despair and melancholy. I am sincere that he will be a great pastor. He knows what people feel when they suffer. He feels their hurt deeply. He is wise and can give them great comfort in their hurts and sorrows. What others feel at times of trials and loss, Daniel feels at times when there are no trials or loss. He has taken great encouragement from the words of Dr. Luther concerning those who suffer this affliction. He has real hope in God's care and love, but it is within him that he cannot always embrace it for himself.

"I say this because he wants so badly to be a pastor, but he could never go away from here to attend school. The changes that would require would overwhelm him. The people here love and respect him. They will accept him as pastor some day. Only I know of his dream, what he feels is his calling. Please, while you are here encourage him that God can make a way for him to become our pastor without the real danger to his mind that going away to school would create. Please, Pastor, nurture him along. Come often and oversee his progress. Serve as our circuit pastor until you assess that he is ready to undertake those duties himself."

Pastor Krueger surveyed the lines of concern in Herr Schmitt's face and the tremble in his voice. His request was highly irregular. But, he felt, nothing is impossible with God. "I will do all that I can, Herr Schmitt. From May to October I can be here once a month. I will observe Daniel. I will encourage him. I will offer him assistance in learning the things necessary. I will do what I can."

Daniel leaned back on the bed and stared at the ceiling. "Katrina, my love, will everything be all right? I know what you have been doing since we were first married. You have encouraged me without prodding and pushing. You have cheered me; really you have, with Scripture and song. You have always been there for me. You have filled my days and nights with joy. Some wives are always visiting at their neighbors. You stay and visit with me. I fear that you will become lonely, but I don't want you to go about as they do. You are a wonderful wife, Katrina, but will everything be all right?"

"You're still worried about someone else coming to teach and then what would you do. That is tomorrow, Daniel. Tomorrow a tornado could wipe out our whole settlement. Tomorrow a passing wagon train could leave us infected with cholera or measles and decimate our town. We can't live in tomorrow, Daniel. God has called you to be a pastor. God will make a way. God has given you clear proof that he wants you to be the teacher in our school. Daniel, God is not mean. He does not trick us or tease us to make us unhappy. He is our shepherd, and we His sheep. I know that things settle deep inside of you. But God dwells there, too. I know you know all these things. You tell them to others when they are hurting. Please, my love, listen as I tell them to you. Come, Daniel, let us sing. Let us sing a song of joy and then pray, and then let us make our own song."

Chapter 32
Daniel: Man and Servant of God

Night had brought no relief from the sweltering heat. The ever more weary citizens of Martinsville arose to find a dawn sun mocking them with the promise of greater agony than the day before. As they plodded to their morning chores a child cried, "Look, Papa, there are two suns this morning." The father shrugged his head in the direction his son pointed. There, on the southern horizon, was a glow brighter than the dawn. "Prairie Fire!" he yelled. "Prairie Fire!"

Adrenalin infused tired bodies as the call was repeated over and over again. Between Martinsville and the fire stood the Platte, but the Platte was low enough for a small child to wade across. With speed and energy beyond the limits of their tired bodies men harnessed horses and hitched the unwilling beasts to the reapers and reaped all the tall prairie grass that stood between them and the river. Others gathered every available bucket or container that could hold water and scooping it from the river ran and placed their buckets at points throughout the settlement. The remaining men hitched other horses to plows and dug deep furrows behind the reapers.

By noon the acrid smell of smoke was beginning to mingle with the smell of sweaty men and animals. Still the villagers toiled to prepare for the raging inferno coming from the south. All the tall grass had been mowed and raked from the land between the village and the river. Now the reapers were mowing and moving the grass to the west of the settlement. The plowmen had finished a furrowed barrier twenty yards wide along the entire southern edge of Martinsville. The goal was to finish a clean swath of land thirty yards wide around the remaining three sides of town and to have at least a five yard barrier of furrows on all those three sides.

Daniel, whose skill with farm machinery was nothing that legends could be made of, had been assigned to organize the water preparations. Knowing the extreme danger that confronted the citizens of his town, and more concerned than that about his beloved Katrina, Daniel ordered the execution of the precious lumber that had been destined as the foundation of his and Katrina's apartment. These cured two by twelve planks had been brought all the way from Council Bluffs, but he and Katrina would not need an apartment if they and everyone else were dead. He had ordered the planks to be cut into lengths of six feet and two feet. From these he made another six troughs for water and placed three at the barn and three at the church.

By two o'clock stray embers had begun falling into the nearly dry riverbed. Daniel ordered that all heavy cloth be brought to the troughs, soaked and put on to roofs. This rapidly depleted the water and tired and crying children were again sent to the river to refill them. As the buckets were returned, Daniel supervised pouring them over the soaked cloth already covering the houses. Back and forth the weary settlers plodded, men in the fields, women and children in town, laboring through extreme exhaustion to save their lives and their community.

By three it was apparent that all the reaping and plowing could not be done before the inferno arrived. Men came in from the field and helped their children collect water from the river. All the buildings were soaked again and again. A little past four the raging storm of flame was just behind the rise over which Pastor Krueger had ridden only a day before. Men gathered their families and they huddled together as the roar of the firestorm shouted at them from across the Platte.

Daniel took a large toolbox and emptied it in the center of town. Turning it upside down he stood upon it and called out above the screaming flames. "Let us pray." The villagers gathered round and Daniel climbed off his box and knelt in the middle of the assembly. Only God and Pastor Krueger who now knelt beside him could hear his words above the roar of the fire. "Almighty God, our Father and Creator of heaven and earth, we have done what we could. It is not enough. Like our salvation from sin, we can never do enough. We cast our fate on your grace, O Lord, and beseech your care for the sheep of your pasture. You alone can preserve us, save us and keep us. Into your hands, Almighty God, we commend our souls for your loving care. Amen." Katrina came and knelt by his other side and the three of them wrapped their arms around each other and waited for God's decision.

Embers fell and sputtered out on the soaked clothing on the roofs. A wave of heat engulfed the settlers as the storm jumped the river and leapt over their buildings and landed on the dry prairie to their north. The wind of the storm carried the sound away with it. Singed but alive the citizens of Martinsville clamored around Daniel praising his efforts and his faith. Daniel, exhausted mentally, physically and emotionally, fell on Katrina's shoulder and wept. Knowing for certain that everyone in town plus Pastor Krueger would now deem him unfit for anything, he pulled himself from his wife's embrace and fled to his house and flung himself in despair on the bed. Katrina sped after him to prevent further disaster.

As the sun set Pastor Krueger, Herr Gelt and Herr Dietrich, his strongest critic, all came to their door. Daniel now sat morosely at the kitchen table, head in his hands, and told Katrina he didn't want to see anyone. Katrina, however, knew better. In his heart he knew she would and that he needed to see whoever had come. The men stood around the table where Daniel sat.

"Herr Cooper," Herr Dietrich began, "we have come to thank you for your labor and sacrifice to save our community." Daniel raised his head a little and looked at Herr Dietrich. He had never called Daniel by a title of respect before.

"Daniel," Pastor Krueger continued the conversation; "your faith and your labor are to be commended. In the history of Martinsville what you have done will always be remembered. In three weeks there will be a church building to dedicate and people to dedicate it. Your labor today has been instrumental in securing both people and property."

"Daniel," Herr Gelt went on, "We all know about the buffalo. We don't care, Daniel. We also all know what you really are made of. Tears, fear and despair swept over us all today. That you hurt more, that is all right. You did not stop until your work was done and then you called us all to seek power above our own. I was so scared, Daniel, that I didn't even think of praying."

"And so was I," added Herr Dietrich. "I was wrong about you Daniel. I will put my children in your school. If you ever again feel overcome then I will hold you and love you as I will my own children who you have saved today."

"Daniel," Pastor Krueger picked up the line of speech, "I will be staying here until the dedication of the new church. Then I will stay another week for the opening of the school. I will lay hands on you and commission you to the work of training the children of Martinsville in the name of our Lord Jesus Christ. In the late spring and summer months I will visit Martinsville as regularly as I can. I will oversee your progress with the children and, if you like, will provide you with books and lessons to better equip you in serving the Lord. Who knows, Daniel, some day you may want to teach adults as well. I can help you prepare for that if you ever want to pursue that idea."

Tears streamed down Daniel and Katrina's cheeks. She rested her hand on his shoulder and he reached up and laid his on top of hers. Speechless he smiled through his tears at the men assembled in his kitchen. Then he stood and firmly shook the hands of the delegation that had come to thank and encourage him.

As the men left Daniel pulled Katrina to him. Holding her tightly he offered a short prayer of thanksgiving. Then holding her at arm's length he laughed. "The devil doesn't have me by the nose and by the toes, dearest Katrina. But try as he might to destroy me, I know he doesn't have me. He has failed and God has prevailed. Oh, he will throw a brick at my head whenever he can. I will still struggle with buffalos that will trample me. I will be filled with all the horrors of hawks and rabbits. I cannot stop those things from happening. They seem a part of me that cannot be altered. But, my beautiful true love, God has given me life and a wonderful wife. With you by my side, loving me, keeping me safe, prodding me ever so gently so I am not supposed to notice, I have hope. Katrina, my dearest love, I have hope." Laughing again he pulled her to him and thought, I am a long way from Wabash.

Notes from Katrina's Journal (Names Amended for Clarity)
School started today. All the children in town were there.

Pastor Krueger was here this week. He offered the sacrament and had Daniel help him.

Daniel has been stricken these past two months by a serious attack of melancholy. Even baby Sarah doesn't cheer him much. But he works on, never missing a responsibility. Even in his own despair he brings me prairie flowers to adorn the table.

Daniel has finished all but one set of lessons given him by Pastor Krueger. He is elated and depressed at the same time. I can only pray that God will preserve him.

Baby Enoch died today. Daniel is nearly immobilized. Still he will come and hold me and assure me that I will be all right. But, O dear God, what about him?

Today Daniel was ordained. What a day of joy and Daniel is not having an attack of melancholy so he has really enjoyed the day. Thank you, God, for a doubly good day.

Adam Gelt has asked to court Sarah. It is a tragedy for Daniel like the hawk and the rabbit. He is beside himself with unnecessary grief. I have had to watch him like a hawk.

Today we had a large celebration. Daniel has been pastor at Hope of Christ for twenty-five years. Sadly he is also in the middle of a buffalo stampede, but he was gracious to all who poured out their thanks to him for his wonderful service. O, Daniel, I want so much for God to give you peace. Someday, my love, He will.

I came into back of the church today. I didn't know Daniel was there. Then I heard the sound of strong weeping at the altar. There he knelt. He was telling God that the recovering from the last buffalo stamped had been the hardest and he didn't think he would ever even try to recover again. He was telling God that it would be easier to just die, even if it meant by his own hand, than to try to pick himself up one more time. He wept out to God about the pain of each stampede growing worse and worse. I slipped out before he noticed me. O God, how can I help him? O God, please help him.

Martinsville is shrinking. No one uses the trail anymore. The train route went north of us by fifteen miles. Tom and Martha are still here but their son has moved the cartage business to Grand Island. Tom is now almost ninety. I don't know if Daniel can stand to do his funeral. Each buffalo stampede lasts longer as he grows older. Still, he is ever faithful to his ministry. In two years we will have a fifty year celebration of Martinsville. Many families will come back for a day, but then leave again. Daniel, O Daniel, can you take it?

Daniel retired today. It was a beautiful service. The district president came and offered the sacrament. We had over one hundred and fifty people come for the day, most of them baptized by Daniel. Daniel has grown into an almost perpetual state of melancholy. Strangely, though, he will still take a long walk out on the prairie and bring me wildflowers. He has always shown me the greatest attention even when he is in his saddest state. The children have given us train tickets to visit them all this summer and fall. I know it won't cheer Daniel, but he will love it even in his melancholy.

Daniel, O Daniel, what will I do without you. You have been my rock, my joy, my only true love. Your gracious heart that beat with love and kindness for so many could just no longer beat. The doctor assures me you died in peace and without any pain. May the peace of God now rest upon you and fill you with an eternity of true happiness. I will see you again soon, dear love.

Chapter 33
Beth

Beth looked at the finished manuscript. What was to be sent to the publisher was done, but she knew that her husband had always kept his own simultaneous back story going. She knew that she must now add her own to finish the tale as well. She quickly sent Daniel's story to the first publisher on her list. She had twenty names of publishers. For her beloved it would have been one rejection and done, but Beth wasn't going to give up. She would find twenty more if necessary. Buffalo Stampede was a story that had to be told. When it was safely in the mail she took her journal and began the completion of her own back story.

Beth put the phone back in its cradle and wiped the tears from her face. They are mistaken, she fumed to herself, if they think I will do their dirty work for them. If they think he can't teach others about peace until he has his own, let them tell him. I won't encourage him to look for a new job so they can hide their hypocrisy. If the church board wants to fire him because he is depressed, they shouldn't look to me to play the fall guy, or gal as it may be.

She walked downstairs to the mailbox and found it stuffed. The envelope containing the manuscript had been returned. One down, a million to go, she sighed. Her husband's newspaper from their previous denomination had arrived that day as well. I don't know why he likes this, she thought. He says it is mostly the columns and news shorts that he likes. Well, let's just see.

Opening to the inside page she found the "Dear Pastor" advice column. "Dear Pastor, our seventeen year old son has just been diagnosed with severe depression. What can you suggest to help?" This should be interesting, she thought. What will he advise? "Dear Brother, I am sorry to hear of this sad diagnosis. Unfortunately at this point you can do nothing. As you have not succeeded in driving the devil out of him by age seventeen, then he is in the devil's grasp forever. I would encourage you to reassess your parenting model for any younger children you still have at home."

Beth sat on the step and reread the article. It wasn't possible that someone had really said that. Reverend Stout had been raised from the dead and was now offering Christian counseling. This was absurd. I can't hide the paper because he knows it comes today. Perhaps it is best to let him see this and finally come to grips with why we left in the first place. Taking the mail upstairs she got out a new envelope and sent the manuscript to publisher number two.

"What is this tripe!" her husband yelled as he slammed the paper down. "Is everyone still locked in medieval pseudo-theology?" He picked up the paper and threw it in the trash. "When our subscription runs out, don't renew it. I'm going for a walk."

Beth sat at the table and cried as he stormed down the stairs. He won't be any happier when the board makes their announcement to him in two months. Two months for me to do their dirty work. Two months for us to have the extra income and a church home. What do they know about peace? All they have created is turmoil and sadness. I've got to do something to help him, find some direction for us to turn, but what?

The next Monday morning Beth was dressed in her most severe outfit. She went to the drugstore and bought a pair of reading glasses with point one magnification. Examining herself in the mirror on the glasses rack she guessed she was as professorial as a twenty year old girl could look. Sliding into the driver's seat of their car she again checked the churches listed in the yellow pages. She knew which ones she didn't have to visit. She knew how they felt already. She reread the questions carefully typed and snapped them securely on the clipboard.

"Good morning, Pastor, my name is Beth. I am a graduate student in psychology at the university and I am doing a survey comparing church's beliefs on certain doctrines and their beliefs on certain aspects of mental illness. Can I please have fifteen minutes of your time?

"First, we will cover the few questions on doctrine. Do you, and does your denomination, believe that the Bible is the absolutely true written word of God?"

"Truth, Beth, is sometimes hard to define. America believes democracy is true. Russia believes communism is true. We would not push either view on our congregations."

"Thank you. Do you and your denomination believe that Jesus Christ was God in the flesh and that salvation can only be found in him?"

"These are rather strange questions for a psychology student. What is salvation? Is it freedom from hunger or sickness? If you are strictly speaking of a 'spiritual salvation', well, how could we be so egocentric to believe that good people all over the world who have their own religious systems are not as equally right as us?"

"Thank you. You are giving me very clear answers. Now I will come to the mental health questions. Do you and your denomination believe that depression is a sin and or a spiritual issue or do you believe it is a real illness in the mind separate from a spiritual only cause?"

"The definition of spiritual is important. You might want to clarify that question when you meet with other clergy. Is depression a sin? Generally, no, although a person who commits a great crime might afterwards feel some remorse and be depressed. The goodness of his spirit rejects the badness of his behavior and that can cause stress and depression. But then we would have to get into a discussion of what sin is and what spiritual is. This is a very wide open question. If we take the traditional view, now widely called into question, of sin and spirit, then absolutely no, sin and depression are not linked. We know much better that mental health issues are caused by chemicals in our minds. I don't know of anyone who would still believe sin as the root cause."

Beth took out the article she had retrieved from the waste basket and showed it to him. He handed it back to her and stated with emphasis, "Poppy cock! Medieval!" At which Beth smiled and thanked him for his time.

One denomination down, nine to go. We could never go here, she thought as she got in the car. That is for sure. Hubby would blow a gasket. She checked it off in the phone book and looked for the address of church number two. Giving the same opening speech she dug right into her first question.

"Absolutely," the pastor ejaculated. "The Bible is true."

"Absolutely," he slammed his palm on his desk. "Christ is God. Not a very popular truth today, but still true. Do you believe it is my question?"

Beth stammered. She hadn't been expecting this. "Well, personally I do, but what I think is not relevant to the survey. Now let's go to the questions on mental illness."

"Of course it is spiritual. Adam sinned and we all suffer the consequences of sin. One of those is depression. You will certainly find it more in the general population than the Christian one. When we trust Christ we become new creatures and things like depression will be left behind. If it isn't readily left behind we would counsel that person to examine their life to see if they have left behind the sins that cause it. Repentance and confession, that's what's needed!"

"Thank you. Now I have just one more question. Would you have someone on your staff if they told you they suffered frequent bouts of depression and often thought of suicide?"

"Absolutely not! Suicide is a terrible sin. Pastors in our denomination are not unanimous in this opinion, but most think suicide is unforgivable. If a person so regularly yields their life to the devil that they are frequently depressed, then there is no way they could serve God. Now, young lady, what are your opinions?"

"It's just a research project, pastor, and I am not supposed to have an opinion in the middle of doing research. It can taint the way I pose the questions." She was very glad that her beloved had a degree in psychology and he had taught her that answer when doing his research. "Thank you very much for your time."

Beth sat at the kitchen table and fought back her tears. In four days she had visited nine churches. Five had similar answers to the first church and the other four to the second church. Two of those churches had been adamant, really almost growled at her in their insistence; depression was a lack of faith. Anybody who had such little faith was not fit for service and if they persisted in their lack of faith were probably not even true believers. If depression did come because of some overwhelming circumstance then they would gladly help that person pray through their troubles. Psychology was part of the problem and she would be better in a different field that might really help someone.

She sighed and lost the battle with her tears. Was there no one who believed the mind was an organ just like every other organ in the body? She had gotten bolder and asked if they thought cancer or diabetes was a sin and that had provoked some strong retorts. Beth buried her face in her arms and sobbed.

"What's the matter, honey?" She was startled that she hadn't heard her husband come in.

She wiped her face. "Nothing. Don't you know that sometimes a woman just has to have a good cry?" She smiled and reached up and kissed him. "Everything is OK," she lied. To herself she added, only seven more weeks until he gets the bad news and I haven't got a good answer yet. What, oh what can I do?

Chapter 34
Beth Perseveres

Daily Beth reviewed her interviews to see if she had missed something, some component of reason or rationale for such positions as had been taken. Daily she prayed that there might be an error or that she had formed the answers she expected by the nature of her questions. Her mind reworked all the lessons her husband had shared about variables in survey outcomes from his own research. Yes, she admitted, I did interject too much of myself and my opinions. No, she further admitted, the questions were not well formed and left too much space for opinion and not concrete answers. But in summation, she thought, none of the consequential answers regarding views of depression had depended on her mistakes.

She buried her head in her arms and tears spilled onto the papers she had been reviewing. Five more weeks, her mind reeled at the shortness of time left, five more weeks and he is done, finished with his ministry and I haven't helped at all. He still has his campus job and graduation is in only a month, but he will be so hurt. O, God, what can I do?

There was one church left on her list. Was it worth it, she debated with herself, to even bother? But I can't say I've done everything if I don't, she rejoined. Will I stop sending manuscripts if I get nine "no's"? No! I'll send a hundred if that's what it takes.

So, I have it figured out, she concluded, I will visit church number ten.

Today she abandoned the pretense of a survey. The church was only two blocks off campus and she walked over to it enjoying the warm spring sunshine. The sign read "Randall McHone, Pastor". Beth went inside, introduced herself and the secretary said she would see if the pastor was busy. He came out of his office and said, "Good morning. How can I help you?"

There was no survey to use as an excuse. She had failed to plan for such a simple question. How could he help? The utter preposterousness of her visit suddenly hit her. Without warning and without will she burst into tears. She wanted to run, run as fast as she could. She wanted to run all the way home to her mother, fall into her arms and bawl her heart out until the end of time. Instead she stood still, tears pouring from her eyes and gulping sobs the only sound she could make.

The secretary gently took her arm and led her to a seat in the pastor's office. Then she took a chair next to her and held her hand. Finally the pastor pulled up another chair and sat facing her. Into her sorrow clouded mind came the first ray of hope. He was not sitting behind his desk. He was open to her. Then he just got up and left but soon returned with a can of soda. "Here," he gently said, "have something to drink. Take all the time you want."

Did she sit there for an hour or a whole morning, she wasn't sure. Would she miss being home to fix her husband lunch, she wasn't sure. She had never missed it. Katrina would never have failed to be there. But she was Beth and this was her problem to solve.

"I'm sorry," she gulped. "It's just that my husband" and then she started to cry again. She felt the gentle squeeze on her hand by the secretary and suddenly realized what it may have sounded like concerning her husband. Pastor McHone continued to sit patiently with a look of genuine concern on his face. Beth pulled herself together, "It's just that my husband is going to lose his job for the stupidest reason!"

Pastor looked at her kindly and said softly, "And what is that reason."

"Because he has depression. They think he can't teach teens about the peace of Christ because he has depression." Her voice rose along with her anger.

Then remembering the questions from her survey she asked, "What do you think, Pastor, is the Bible true?"

"Absolutely," he smiled kindly.

Beth accepted another tissue from the secretary. "Then do you believe that Jesus is God and that we can only be saved through him?"

The pastor nodded and replied, "Absolutely."

The last church of his denomination she had been to hadn't been sure on the first point but fairly sure on the second. This pastor was absolutely sure on both. Encouraged by his kindness and his answers she jumped to the last question. "Would you ever let a person who suffered from depression serve in your church?" Now she waited for the bombshell that always fell.

"Depression can be a very serious illness, Beth. Some people have it for short periods and some people just have it. Dr. Luther, the founding teacher of Lutheranism, may have had it himself. He was certainly gentle with and understanding of those who did have it. I am sure he would never have made it a litmus test for ministry."

Beth sniffled and blew her nose. "Actually, I know quite a bit about what Dr. Luther taught on the subject. My husband is also an author. He wrote a book on the problems people with depression face in serving in the church. He has his main character become a Lutheran. But do all Lutherans believe like you do about the Bible and salvation?"

"Sadly, they do not. Years ago in Germany a field of criticism about the Bible became a popular area of study for Lutherans. Gradually it came to America and has slowly crept into some of our denominations. Our denomination, the Missouri Synod, steadfastly rejects this form of criticism. So, no, all Lutherans are not on the same page about all things.

"Tell me a little about your husband's book."

Beth told him much more than a little bit. "But his background is so not Lutheran that I don't think he would ever follow Daniel in becoming one. But now the church board is going to fire him and what then? Where can he serve and be happy?"

"Well, it happens that I am also a chaplain in the Air Force and know a good deal about many other Christian denominations. I can recommend a few to you that might be very kind and understanding. Of course we would love to have you embrace Lutheranism, but we'll wait until God's time for that to happen. Let me just say to you, Beth, that with a wife like you, your husband will have great success in whatever ministry he undertakes." He went to his desk and wrote down the names of several denominations that Beth had not explored.

"Now, Beth, let me have a word of prayer with you." Pastor McHone's prayer washed over her mind like a cooling waterfall of hope. Someone had cared about her and her husband. She hadn't been cajoled or ridiculed or had to hear a denial of Christ. She thanked him and found herself giving both he and his secretary a warm hug. Clutching her list of hope she went home to fix lunch. It really hadn't taken that long after all, she thought. But now I have hope.

The next five weeks sped past. She had not given her husband any inkling of the meeting he would face the next night at church. She prayed for him and prayed over her list of hope. Wednesday afternoon came and Beth's anxiety rose in contradiction to her prayers for peace. A sad emptiness hung heavy in her chest as she went downstairs to get the mail. There was only a large manila envelope. "No!" she screamed in her mind and hoped it hadn't really echoed through the apartment house. No, not another rejection.

Sadly she trudged back up the stairs and emptied the contents of the envelope into another one. She sat at her husband's typewriter and wrote another letter of introduction. Using her tears to wet the glue on the envelope she sealed it and sent it off to another publisher. Then, hoping to cheer herself and her mate she prepared a meal that she knew was one of his favorites.

Her husband came home from work and plopped wearily on the sofa. "Boy am I tired," he sighed. "I wish I didn't have that meeting tonight. I would rather just collapse. And I still have one paper left to write, too."

Beth sat down beside him. "Is there anything I can do to help? Do you have a rough draft of your paper I can type?" He shook his head. "Well, I can do one thing. I made monkey brains for supper."

"Really!" He exclaimed. "It's been ages. You know that is how I survived eating as a bachelor. Monkey brains every night. I'm starving. Is it ready?" Beth kissed his forehead and they trouped to the kitchen for supper.

They ate in relative silence, each absorbed with thoughts they did not wish to share. Keeping his mouth full of his favorite food was an adequate excuse for his silence. When he finally pushed aside his dish Beth reached across and took his hand. "I have some news for you. Some is good, but some is bad. Which do you prefer first?"

"Is the bad news that I am going to be dismissed from youth director tonight?" He saw the shock of awareness in her eyes. "Bernie called me and gave me a heads up. He asked if I would just resign quietly so they didn't have to take it up. 'No embarrassment for you that way' he said to me. There will be no embarrassment for me anyway I told him. I have done nothing wrong to be embarrassed about. You thought I was great and capable before you learned of my serious depression and now you think I am not. I will not be the one embarrassed."

"You didn't really say that, did you?"

"Yes, I did. I have just had it. I can be my own freak and I can be your special freak, but I am not just going to play the freak for everyone. I just let out my comment before I even thought of what I should say. Bernie seemed rather taken aback. How long have you known?"

Beth hung her head and told him eight weeks. "You are so busy and I just didn't want to tell you. You graduate in a month anyway and we will be moving. It's not the end of the world, especially if you really feel like you told Bernie."

"I do indeed. But, dear love, it just is one more door of opportunity that is shut. I really don't know where to turn next."

"Well, that is my good news. I went for a walk today and went past the Lutheran church on the hill. I saw the pastor and he was just so nice I told him everything about our situation. Don't jump to any conclusions. I'm not going to say we should become Lutherans. But he did say that everything you had put in your book is what his kind of Lutherans still believe. Apparently they all don't, but his kind do. Anyway, he is also a chaplain in the reserves and so he knows a lot about other denominations. He gave me a list of other groups that would be open to you serving there. Some of them would even accept your correspondence degree from seminary. It means that there may be hope of ministry still in our future."

He stood up from the table and pulled Beth up to him. "I love you, Beth. Thank you. Hope is good. You know that you are the dearest on earth to me and that with you I know I have hope. The buffalo may stampede, the hawks may kill rabbits, I may fall and fail, but Christ has given you to me for hope. Pastor Combes was all wrong. You will help me to succeed." Beth rested her head against his shoulder. The young man stroked her long brown hair, kissed the top of her head and whispered, "Hope is good."

www.ingramcontent.com/pod-product-compliance
Lightning Source LLC
Chambersburg PA
CBHW070111290526
45789CB00005B/1998